TALES FROM THE
HARDWOOD
SURVIVING & THRIVING

101
LEADERSHIP
LESSONS, STORIES, &
MOMENTOUS EXPERIENCES
FROM MY TIME ON
THE COURT

ANDREW MAROTTA

Copyrighted Material

Tales from the Hardwood Surviving & Thriving: 101 Leadership Lessons, Stories, & Momentous Experiences from My Time on the Court

Copyright © 2022 by Andrew Marotta LLC. All Rights Reserved.

No part of this publication may be reproduced, stored in a retrieval system or transmitted, in any form or by any means—electronic, mechanical, photocopying, recording or otherwise—without prior written permission from the publisher, except for the inclusion of brief quotations in a review.

For information about this title or to order other books and/or electronic media, contact the publisher:
Andrew Marotta
www.andrewmarotta.com
andrewmarottallc@gmail.com

ISBN: 978-0-9990055-2-1 (print)
       978-0-9990055-3-8 (eBook)

Printed in the United States of America
Cover and Interior design: 1106 Design
Cover photo: Keith Morris

To my wife Jenn,

I want to thank you for all the love and support you showed over the years. You were there for me and our family when I was gone. All those nights in the winter when I was at the games, nights in the spring when I was at the tryouts, the nights in the summers when I was at the camps, and the nights in the fall when I was at the conferences. During those times, you raised our children, cared for them, and showed them love in my absence. You brought them to the gyms and arenas and chased them around the seats, trying keep them from running onto the court, especially when they were yelling for daddy. You took them out of some arenas when it got bad, especially in Philadelphia! (I love you, Philly, but you scared my kids!) It was a great run for 20 years, and I enjoyed it all. I look forward to the next chapter with you. Thanks for everything: calming me before the games and listening to me after. The travel, the late nights, the laundry, the phone calls, and most importantly, the love and dedication you showed all those years. I love you. #MTC

TABLE OF CONTENTS

Acknowledgments		xi
Foreword by John Feinstein		xv
Introduction		xxi
Chapter 1:	Firsts	1
	1. Here are our ACC refs for today, three of the best.	1
	2. I have never been to Wichita in my life!	3
	3. Pregnant and late.	5
	4. Welcome to Notre Dame!	8
	5. Hey, do you want to ref this afternoon?	10
	6. First flight.	11
	7. Andrew, sorry about your Dad.	14
	8. We're not gonna take any s%$# tonight!	16
	9. Stand tall.	18
Chapter 2:	Points of Leadership	21
	10. Never miss a chance to let them see you shine.	21
	11. Be the best team on the court, by Ron Bertovich	23
	12. In it for the long haul.	24
	13. It's time, by Roger Ayers.	25

	14. Know something about the people/the event before you arrive.	27
	15. The fax.	28
	16. Leadership, by John Clougherty.	31
	17. "I'm going to hire my officials from the social."	33
	18. It's the Garden, kid.	35
	19. Impact, by John Adams.	37
	20. Same play the same way.	39
	21. Be the ref everyone wants to work with.	40
	22. You can't do it all by yourself, by Dr. Harold Abraham	41
	23. Stay in your area.	42
Chapter 3:	Failure to Success	45
	24. Who is the foul on?	45
	25. Not straight at all.	48
	26. You're not even on the list.	49
	27. So bad he ripped his pants.	51
	28. Give a warning.	53
	29. The toss.	55
	30. Next play.	57
	31. Best write-up ever.	58
	32 If you have been doing this long enough…	61
	33. I'm sorry, Coach.	62
	34. Whanua, by Steve Donahue.	64
Chapter 4:	Hard Work	67
	35. Why are you down here for scrimmages?	67
	36. Get out there and do it.	69
	37. You never know who is watching.	70
	38. How did you get here?	72
	39. Invest the money and the time.	74
	40. Now go work 1000 games.	75

Table of Contents

	41. Patience, by Gary Duda.	76
	42. Take great notes.	78
	43. Make it look easy.	79
Chapter 5:	Communication	81
	44. The beautiful brunette.	81
	45. Take a deep breath, and have fun.	83
	46. Attention to detail.	85
	47. Presence.	86
	48. The game within the game.	87
	49. Tell me what you saw.	89
	50. Why curse like that?	90
	51. Reach out.	91
	52. Good job.	92
	53. You're damn right someone is going to get hurt.	92
	54. Put the pasta in.	94
	55. Acceptance, by Brandon Cruz.	95
	56. Are we good?	98
	57. Don't f%$# it up!	99
	58. Points of emphasis.	100
	59. The wise old man, by Andrew Maira.	101
Chapter 6:	Truths	105
	60. Check the tape.	105
	61. Perception.	107
	62. I'm not as bad as what they told you.	108
	63. Excuses: the flat tire.	109
	64. For two years you are number one with me.	112
	65. Mark it!	114
	66. Andrew, I'm sorry. I know better than that.	115
	67. New game, new day.	118
Chapter 7:	Mentorship	121
	68. It's your call, kid.	121

	69. Shoulder to shoulder.	124
	70. Bring in the cooler.	126
	71. Now we can play.	129
	72. I saw you last night.	131
	73. Money out of your wallet.	134
	74. You're on scholarship tonight, kid.	136
	75. What can I do to get better?	137
	76. Give him a chance, Coach.	139
	77. There is a reason why they are called legends, by Dan Spainhour.	140
	78. Wow, you held the ball.	142
Chapter 8:	Mental Strength	145
	79. The brighter the lights.	145
	80. You don't have to ref the whole game.	147
	81. Just another game.	148
	82. The last season.	149
	83. Be at your best on a Tuesday night.	152
	84. Mental strength and performance.	153
	85. The quiet.	155
	86. Bench time.	156
	87. What's your best game?	157
	88. Blue and white.	158
	89. Why did you give him an A rating?	159
	90. Get right back in there and ref your a$% off.	160
	91. Be where your feet are.	161
	92. Only blow if you know.	163
Chapter 9:	Be Ready	165
	93. The play is coming to me.	165
	94. The knock at the door.	166
	95. Hey, kid, will you park my car?	168
	96. The elbow.	169
	97. Mom's watching.	171

Table of Contents

	98. Hot dog.	173
	99. Act as if.	176
	100. Big call, big stage, big confidence, by Jose Anibal Carion.	177
Chapter 10:	Absorb the Chaos	179
	101. Absorbing chaos, by J.D. Collins.	179
Conclusion		183
About the Author		185

ACKNOWLEDGMENTS

I'd like to thank the many, many mentors, friends, and family who were part of this amazing journey of leadership, growth, and officiating. The game of college basketball is a great one, and I was proud to be part of it, wearing the stripes for almost twenty years. Many of the stories in *Tales from the Hardwood* are from my experiences and interactions with others: what they did for me, what I learned from them, and how they shone through in tough, tense experiences. I admired them, learned from them, and put into practice many of the habits and strategies they used to be successful on and off the court.

I am grateful to John Feinstein for his mentorship and guidance in becoming an author and for writing the foreword. John has always been a friend to the refs and respects their part in the game.

I am extremely thankful to the many supervisors who believed in me over the years and hired me into the leagues they supervise, especially the great John Clougherty. John is one of the best in the game in many areas and gave me an amazing opportunity to officiate at some of the highest levels.

Tales from the Hardwood: Surviving and Thriving

Big thanks to all listed here who participated and shared their experiences of leadership and learning by writing an anecdote in the book:

Dr. Harold Abraham	*John Clougherty*
John Adams	*J.D. Collins*
Roger Ayers	*Brandon Cruz*
Ron Bertovitch	*Steve Donahue*
Chris Caputo	*Gary Duda*
Jose Anibal Carrion	*Andrew Maira*
Dr. Francis Celis	*Daniel Spainhour*
Nick Chuckran	

I didn't define what they could write about other than it should be leadership related and must be able to help others. I appreciate the uniqueness of each story and hope you will benefit from their participation. I am thankful to them all and overwhelmed by their amazing experiences.

I'd like to thank my family: Jennifer, Claire, Matt, and Tessa for the time to write and the many hours away to complete this project. Thanks to my Mom for coming to so many games over the years and being my biggest fan. I cherish our memories together.

Thank you to Nancy and Rebecca up in Kerhonkson, New York, for hosting my writing retreats where I wrote most of the book. You have a beautiful place.

Shout out to Coach Tom Rickard, who helped with the cover for two books in a row and to Keith Morris for taking the cover photo. The picture was taken on the esteemed *Paul Rickard Court* in Middletown, New York.

Acknowledgments

I tried to be as accurate as I could with the dates and locations of the events, but some could be off. The stories are spot on!

Lastly, thank you to *you* for reading the book. It is my hope that I can help you in your leadership journey by sharing the experiences and stories in *Tales from the Hardwood*. It was a fun ride. #Enjoy and keep rolling.

FOREWORD

By John Feinstein

Although the rumor that I was there when James Naismith hung the first peach basket in 1890 is completely untrue, I have been around basketball for a *long* time.

During those years, I've been fortunate to know many referees. The best ones—like my friend Andrew Marotta—have a number of things in common. One of them is this: When they talk about coaches, they say, "I enjoy working for him." Or, in some cases, "He can be tough to work for."

The point is this: they see themselves as working *for* the coaches and *for* the players. They know they aren't stars and that people don't pay to watch them referee. I should pause here to say I've known *some* refs who *do* think people pay to watch them ref, but they are few and far between.

To be a good basketball referee, in addition to taking the approach that you are working *for* those involved in the game and *for* the sport itself, you have to be in good shape; you have to be a team player; you have to learn to put your ego aside—especially at crucial moments—and you have to walk off the court feeling good if no one has noticed your work for 40 minutes or more (for the record, referees and sportswriters do *not* get paid overtime). The most important quality of the best referees is that they are leaders, on and off the court. They demonstrate and model leadership in all they do.

Let's take the necessities of being a good official one at a time:

Being in shape: That's pretty apparent. Basketball is the toughest sport there is to officiate. You have to be prepared to run the court for 40 minutes and make calls that are almost never easy—there's no harder call to make in sports than the block/charge. You don't sit down during timeouts, and you don't get subbed for if you're tired.

Being a team player: I've been lucky enough to sit with officials in their pre-game meetings. They are all about detail: How to position as the lead or as the middle or as the trail; who is responsible for what calls; how to back one another up—especially after a technical foul, when everyone's adrenaline is high. They talk about coaches' personalities and helping one another out if things get tense.

I remember Tom Fraim, who worked in the ACC for 23 years, saying one night: "If I have to tee someone up, make sure I walk to the right foul line. If I'm wound up, I might go in the wrong direction."

Putting your ego aside: All that matters is getting every call right, not proving that you're in charge. Often, you'll see an official with a better angle run in and talk to an official who has made a call that might be wrong. The good ones trust their partners: almost always, the second guy has the call right.

There is also the concept of invisibility. The less often an official gets noticed, the better. The good ones avoid getting into shouting matches with coaches, they know when to say, "Enough" and when to walk away. They also know there are times you admit a mistake—officials make them the same way coaches, players, and even sportswriters make them.

Hank Nichols, the Hall-of-Fame referee, used to say to coaches after he missed a call: "I missed it; I owe you one—but I'll never pay it back." In other words, you don't correct a mistake with a makeup call—you just try to get the next one right.

On the night that the University of Maryland's Cole Field House closed, I was standing in the runway leading from the locker rooms to the court when the officials walked by me. John Clougherty (featured in *Tales from the Hardwood* and Andrew's mentor), the lead ref that night, who I had known for years, stopped to chat for a minute. As he left, he gave me a quick hug, the way friends will do.

Tom Boswell, my long-time *Washington Post* colleague, was standing a few feet away. "You *hug* referees?" he said, clearly shocked. "Boz," I answered, "they're good guys and good sources. They always know what's going on." Tom nodded and said, "That makes sense."

The last and most important quality of the best officials is *leadership*. That is what this book is all about. Leadership. Stories, examples, strategies, techniques, and more from great officials and even better leaders. They are fathers, friends, brothers, and more. They have failed on the court and in life, yet through some crazy resilience, they keep showing up night after night. This book is not for officials only but for anyone on their journey of leadership. Anyone looking to grow in their personal and professional lives who wants great tips and experiences of leadership, on and off the court, written by a great storyteller and Division I official. Andrew makes these examples come alive through a variety of ways in this writing.

Tales from the Hardwood: Surviving and Thriving

I had the chance to watch Andrew Marotta work for years and got to know him well. I think we bonded through being New Yorkers and loving basketball. Andrew has all the qualities I mentioned above to be a great referee and leader. I could see his leadership from being a HS Principal while he was on the floor: taking charge in difficult situations, his body language and communication, and overall presence on the court. In addition, he always went out of his way to try to mentor younger officials, remembering those who mentored him when he was breaking into the business.

Andrew is a leader and educator. These two roles helped make him a better official. He enjoyed dealing with young people, helping them do their job—in this case, play basketball—as well as they possibly could. He has focused a lot of his life on teaching and on leadership—not just being a leader, but teaching others how to lead. He masterfully combines these topics and more into this book, creating an engaging experience for the reader who may be looking to grow in leadership and not just in officiating. This book is so much more.

He's taught me a lot about basketball through the years. My guess is this book will teach a lot of people a lot about basketball and about leadership. Enjoy the ride.

—*John Feinstein*

John Feinstein is a New York Times *best-selling author and award-winning sportswriter for the* Washington Post. *He has written almost 50 books. He is a master storyteller. Feinstein is a contributor for ESPN, NPR, a podcast host, and a TV broadcaster. A college-basketball junkie, in love with golf, and a baseball fanatic. John has always been a friend to the refs and wants the best for the game. Thank you, John, for the perfect "opening tip" to* Tales from the Hardwood.

INTRODUCTION

From my first freshmen league games in Staten Island, New York, to Cameron Indoor, the Carrier Dome, the Palestra, the Dean Dome, and more, I have learned along the way. Each and every game, trip, video review, official meeting, I learned. I can remember two kids crashing into each other in a small HS gym my first season and thought to myself, *Oh, that is a foul*...and quickly realized it was *me* who was supposed to blow the whistle. From that experience to the tidal wave of boos and profanities in a 20,000-seat arena when a call went against the home team. I quickly learned why the word *fan* came from the word *fanatic*.

It all started out as just basketball and officiating, but somewhere along the journey, it turned into so much more. I found myself being, acting, and speaking more confidently. I found myself making examples of something that happened at a game and relating to my role as a school leader, or even a father or husband. I was in better shape, dressed better, was more organized, focused, and more. I found myself communicating better and being able to "read the room," as my wife calls it, knowing when to engage with someone and when to leave it alone and create space.

Tales from the Hardwood: Surviving and Thriving

I met and befriended many mentors and made countless friends on this journey, some of whom are featured in this book. My good friend Dr. Rob Gilbert, Montclair St. University Sports Psychologist, always says that *Success leaves clues,* and so many people have done this for me: modeled and passed on tips, strategies, and winning habits to me that I still have today. Again, they may have started out as tips for being a successful college basketball official, but they became much more.

I have used the stories, lessons, and strategies that you will find in this book in many leadership situations. I find them to be invaluable, personal, and important to me in my leadership journey, and now I pass them on to you. Whether you're a parent, school leader, business professional, doctor, lawyer, or whatever your line of work is, these leadership points can touch your heart and your mind, and impact your actions in many ways.

Enjoy. Read. Share the stories. Practice them yourself. Reach out to me on Twitter @andrewmarotta21 and let me know how they helped you. I am proud of my time as a college basketball official from 2001 to 2019, and I'm excited to share the stories, lessons, and more with you.

1

FIRSTS

The truth shall set you free.
—John 8:32

1. Here are our ACC refs for today, three of the best.
Fall, 2010, inter-squad scrimmage, Dean Dome, Chapel Hill, North Carolina

This was my first time at the University of North Carolina, located in beautiful Chapel Hill, North Carolina. The Tarheels play in the Dean Smith Center, named after their Hall of Fame and legendary coach, Dean Smith. It was just an inter-squad scrimmage with no crowd or any fanfare, but I was excited. I'd grown up watching the light-blue Tarheels, including the great Michael Jordan while he was there. I was honored to be there.

We came out onto the court in our informal stripes and shorts and stretched on the side, while the players ran through reps on the court during practice. Traditionally, the coach would blow the whistle, and look to start the scrimmage. There usually was minimal to no talking ahead of time, but rather just getting going with the contest. Not today. Hall of Fame Coach Roy Williams blew the whistle, called the team, managers, and coaches together, as well as us into the huddle. He spoke to the team and about his expectations for the next sixty minutes and went over some specifics. He then introduced the three officials. Now, keep in mind, I had not met him yet (he knew the other two officials, but it was my first time there); we had never said hello, shook hands, or anything.

He said, "This is Joe _____, Mike _____, and Andrew Marotta. They are three of the top ACC officials. If they speak to you today about a call, you listen. They are here to get in shape themselves but also here as ambassadors of the game and can help us get better and learn." Coach Williams then shook our hands, and the players came over also.

I tried to hold my jaw up from hitting the floor. In just those few sentences, Coach Williams had done the following:

- *Raised our stock with his team.*
- *Set a level of expectation of behavior of his players toward the refs.*

- *Showed he knew us by name. He was not reading off a paper and spoke as if he'd known me for a long time.* ***It was my first time there!***

Leadership Takeaway: I was blown away by Coach Williams with just that short interaction. It was such a display of leadership. The fact that an ACC head coach who has countless things to do, know, attend to, create, implement, etc. knew my name prior to a scrimmage game really impressed me. Did an assistant give it to him minutes before? Did he check it on an informational sheet moments earlier? Who cares! When he spoke to the team and us, it was informative, assertive, and personal. Probably no one else in the arena saw what he did because it looked so natural, but he caught my attention, for sure.

It is important to get the big things right, but it starts with the little things—as simple as knowing someone's name. He also didn't just say my name. He told his team, the coaches, the managers all that I was one of the best ACC refs. He established credibility in one quick sentence.

When you have people coming to your school or organization, make the simple effort of getting their names and learning something about them. This story exemplifies how much equity it creates in the hearts and minds of those you are working with.

---

2. I have never been to Wichita in my life!

November 15, 2009, Fairleigh Dickinson University vs. Wichita State, Wichita, Kansas.

It was my first time out in Kansas. I love visiting places I've never been to, and I also really liked when the college basketball team was the only show in town—that is, the city did not have a professional team. Wichita, Kansas, was one of those places. Their men's college basketball team was historically very good, including getting to the Final Four twice, most recently in 2013. They were playing Fairleigh Dickinson University from Teaneck, New Jersey, located not far from the George Washington Bridge, which connects northern New Jersey and New York.

This was one of the games where the home team is supposed to win; the better team actually *pays* the opponent to come to their arena because it is mostly like a guaranteed win. They call these games "guaranteed" games or "pay" games. It is viewed as a necessary way of business in the NCAA and a win-win. The home team gets a win, builds confidence for their team, and maybe gets some players who might not play a whole lot, some more playing experience. The visitor helps build up their budget for their school, helps in recruiting because they can tout all the places they travel, and their players can have some experience of playing at a higher level and on a larger stage.

The game quickly was getting out of hand fast, and Fairleigh Dickinson (FDU) was clearly outmatched. Wichita State was dominating them early in every facet of the game. The coach for FDU, of Italian descent, started to act out and get out of line. I tried a few techniques to calm him, assure him he was getting a fair shake. None worked.

He began screaming things like, "I know how this works! I know I'm the road team, and you'll never see me again. You're a homer. We're getting screwed!" I had to put a stop to this. I beelined to him, went almost nose to nose, and asked firmly, "What is the matter?" He continued in the same vein that he was getting screwed because he was the road team, that I was favoring the home team because I work their league, etc. I boldly proclaimed, *"COACH, calm down! I don't know what you are talking about. Listen! I live twenty minutes from FDU, I've never been to Kansas before, and you and I might be the only two Italians in this arena (just kidding, Kansas!), so calm down and work with me. No one here is trying to screw you!"*

His jaw dropped and for the first time that night, he was speechless. He grabbed both my arms and pleaded with me, "Thank you, *Thank you!*" We remained in close contact throughout the rest of the game while they got their butts kicked!

Leadership Takeaway: Know your surroundings, know your guests, know your personnel, and find relatable points between or among you. Once that coach could relate to me, he felt an instant connection. In just one sentence, I firmly gave him three relatable connections that put him at ease. He especially liked the Italian joke! He stopped blaming me for his team's failures and saw me as an ally. While you can't win 'em all over, you certainly can try to bring them at least a little closer to you and your camp. Use your skills, instincts, and all your resources to help you communicate effectively.

3. Pregnant and late.

November 18, 2005, University of New Hampshire vs. Columbia University, New York, New York

Man, was I nervous. My first Division I at the college level. I am not a nervous person by nature, but I was nervous on that day. My wife, Jennifer, took the one-and-a-half-hour ride down with me to NYC. We had some light conversation, and she was supporting me (like she always has) by listening and being present. About halfway down from Northeast Pennsylvania, we stopped for coffee and gas. At the checkout, I casually asked Jenn, "Hey—did you get the results back from the pregnancy test?"

We had been trying to get pregnant for a few months. She looked at me with a million emotions in her face: joy, fear, happiness, holding back tears, straight-face, etc. She didn't even have to say a word. We/she were pregnant! WOW! Amazing. I was thrilled. We embraced, she cried, my heart pounded, and I forgot all about the game for a short while. My mind was racing: the game, a baby…I am like a real grown-up with responsibility. I felt a sense of warmth, confidence, and love come over me. I was exhilarated.

New York City is always busy, and I always leave plenty of time for some sort of traffic delay, an accident…something. Columbia had a tiny garage beneath the arena where you were directed to park. We arrived plenty early, parked, and sat in the car quietly for a short while. Then we went to a cafe, and then on to the arena. Back then, you had to be there two hours prior to the game, so I was thirty minutes early, arriving at 4:30 pm.

I met my one partner in the locker room about 4:50 pm, and then the supervisor arrived, the late, great Mickey Crowley. Mickey was a long-time, legendary New York ref from Long Island. He oozed personality and charm and was beloved. He warmly greeted us, congratulated me on my first game, told me not to f*$% it up, and then asked where our third partner was. Neither of us knew—nor had we heard from him. Mickey quickly lost his smile, pointed at me, and said to get him on the phone. I got him on the phone and awkwardly talked between Mickey and my partner, encouraging him to get down to the locker room. It was his first game, too, and he had missed the instructions about the parking garage and was looking for parking (the greatest challenge in New York City!) Mickey was not happy.

The third ref arrived at approximately 5:30 pm, thirty minutes late. Mickey was pacing by the door. He didn't say a word in front of us when the ref walked in, he just pointed to the door. They went out and Mickey let him have it...yelling, cursing...a tongue lashing I was not expecting. Tough way to start the game for him and the crew.

Leadership Takeaway: There were so many "firsts" in this story. So many lessons, so many emotions. The point is that *you can handle it all.* You can do it. My first game, first being told that my wife was pregnant, my first meeting with the supervisor, and the first time I witnessed a ref getting chewed out for being late (it was intense and tense!). I breathed deeply, tried to slow it all down, and compartmentalize:

- *My wife was going to be pregnant for many more months, so that could wait.*
- *The other guy being late was not my business. I wasn't late, so shake that off.*
- *You were hired to do this job. He (Mickey) selected me, so go do the job.*

- *It was only two hours. Focus, follow my training, and work hard.*

These short mindsets helped me get through the rollercoaster of emotions that had happened in just the previous two hours. It all worked out, thankfully, but if I hadn't been able to set aside those other events and focus on the job in front of me, it could have been a very short run at the Division I level. I remember this day so vividly and was grateful for it all!

4. Welcome to Notre Dame!

November 1, 2014, University of Minnesota-Duluth vs. Notre Dame (exhibition) South Bend, Indiana.

I tell this story often when I present to schools and principals. I heard the renowned education leader Jimmy Casas use the term, "Director of First Impressions," and it fits perfectly for this story. Like many of the stories in this chapter, it was my first time officiating at Notre Dame. I was excited and proud to be at such a prestigious university refereeing. I chuckled as I drove close to the school thinking about some of the places I refereed where I was banging on the outside of the gym door and a custodian would open the door, asking what I was doing there, and I'd have to explain that I was there to ref the game, and he didn't even know there was a game!!!

As I approached the outer parking lot, I saw a parking attendant. She waved me over and greeted me warmly, "Hi, I'm Ashley. Welcome to Notre Dame." I told her I was one of the officials for the game, and she directed me to her colleague Mike, who was deeper in the web of parking lots. Mike said, "Welcome to Notre Dame" and shared that I was in spot number three adjacent to the sidewalk. Next to spot number three was Mike's colleague Tara, who removed the cone and walked me into the spot like the guide at the airport for the planes as they pull into the gate. As you might guess, Tara greeted me with a smile saying, "Welcome to Notre Dame!" I thanked her, and she walked me to the outer door of the arena, where she introduced me to Robert. She said, "Robert will take you to the locker room." You might guess what Robert said. You bet: "Welcome to Notre Dame, Andrew."

Robert and I had some friendly small talk as we walked through the large hallways. As we approached the locker room door, I actually said out loud, "No way." Sure enough, outside the locker room door was an older gentleman in a green suit and hat, who boldly greeted me in a loud Irish brogue (stretching out the Weeeelllllcoome), "Welcome to Notre Dame!"

Leadership Takeaway: Sounds so simple, but it is the fact that this occurred in this fashion that was amazing. Someone in leadership at that institution directed these folks to greet everyone with, "Welcome to Notre Dame." I loved it and felt so welcome. As I reflected on the awesomeness of this welcome, I shared it with my secretaries at my school in Port Jervis, New York. They laughed, and I told them I wanted each person to be greeted with, "Welcome to Port Jervis High School." You can't go wrong with that greeting, and, like Jimmy Casas shared in his talk, be the director of first impressions: Notre Dame certainly did this, and I urge you to think about how those arriving at your school or organization are treated.

5. Hey, do you want to ref this afternoon?

July 1995, University Basketball Camp (UBC), St. Clare's Church, Staten Island, New York

It was the summer between my sophomore and junior year of college, and I was a proud counselor/coach at the esteemed University Basketball Camp run by the legends Gela and Greg Mikalauskas. Gela and Greg ran a great camp not only teaching basketball to kids, but teaching the young counselors how to act, be professional, and give their best through the hot summers.

One day, Greg asked, "Hey, Andy (the Mikalauskas family were the only people who were allowed to call me "Andy" because of fun camp traditions!), "do you want to ref a scrimmage game this afternoon?" I said, "I have never reffed." He said confidently, "You know the game. You're tough. I think you'd be great. $20 with your name on it if you can do it." I was in.

Leadership Takeaway: The power of a single experience. The power of a single interaction. Answering a certain way to one question. As soon as I put that whistle around my neck, and blew the first few plays of the game, I was exhilarated. I felt a total sense of control and peace with the game. I loved it, until Greg barked at me because of a play he didn't like. *Whaaat?* I thought to myself. *This is my mentor, friend, and the guy who hired me, and he is yelling at me? How is this right?* While I was startled by the yelling, I got over it pretty quick because I loved the position of referee.

That single experience planted the seed for me to become an official after college. Greg provided an opportunity to me, and I took it. In reflecting on that monumental moment in my life, I think about:

- *The power of taking risks and chances.*
- *Be around good people. Good things will come.*
- *Say "Yes" to opportunities.*
- *Believe that you can do it. Most times you can.*
- *You don't know what you don't know unless you try it.*

I am grateful to Greg and Gela for the opportunities they gave me over the years. More importantly, the leadership lessons I learned from them and UBC as a college kid working a camp were invaluable. They are great friends and leaders in basketball and beyond. Say "Yes" to opportunities when they come your way. If I had not liked it, that would have been OK, and I just would not have done it again. There is *power* in "Yes." *Opportunity* in "Yes,"—and maybe a book one day!

6. First flight.

February 17, 2007, Old Dominion University (ODU) vs. Toledo, Toledo, Ohio.

Wow. I had always dreamed of this. Flying to a game. #Bigtime. This is what the big-timers did all the time, and I wanted to be like them. Being whisked away on a plane, reffing the game, and jumping back on the plane to the next contest. It sounds so easy and romantic. Sounds so smooth and enjoyable.

Not exactly.

My original plan was to drive to Toledo. It was a little less than eight hours away. It was a Saturday night game, so I could leave late Friday after school, and arrive in plenty of time on Saturday to relax and prep for the game. Drive a few hours after the game Saturday night, drive again early Sunday, and be home in time to meet my family for church. No problem.

There had been a huge storm on Valentine's day, just a few days earlier. I had heard of some issues on the interstates, but this game would be days later, and all would be fine (so I thought.) I wasn't even close to I-78 west junction when I hit a standstill. Traffic stopped dead. My GPS started going crazy, and there were massive delays. I was close to the Allentown/Bethlehem Lehigh Valley Airport (ABE). I made some crazy u-turns, drove over a divider and a curb, and made my way to the airport. I had to get to the game!

Check out the local newspaper describing the roads:

I called my wife and asked her to book me on the next flight to Detroit ASAP. She (supporting me once again) made a conference call with me and the flight agent, and there was a flight leaving in approximately thirty minutes. I sped through the terminal pickup area, sprinted up to the counter, handed the agent my phone and credit card, drove to the closest parking spot (the one-hour pick-up waiting area...mistake) and sprinted back to the counter. Remember, I was planning on driving, so I was not prepared to fly:

not dressed professionally, bag not organized to fly, and just not ready for it at all. My wife and the agent booked me, she printed my ticket, and off I went.

Security! I had my handy dandy LeatherMan in my bag (the best multi-purpose tool). The agents said there were no lockers and there was nothing they could do. Damn! I had minutes to get to the gate. I sprinted to the exits, looked at the huge snow banks to the left and right of the walkways, and jammed the LeatherMan into the snow. Sweating like a madman, I got through security and to the gate with just seconds to spare and got to Detroit that night.

Leadership Takeaway: It ain't easy. It might look easy, and, many times, things go your way, but my first flying experience was not a good one. I was so frazzled and turned upside down. When my head hit the pillow that night, I was spent. I knew I had a tough game in a new environment (ODU won by three in a tight game on the road), and I had to focus and settle in.

You play the hands you are dealt. Try to control the controllables as best you can, but sometimes things will go sideways. How could the interstates still have been blocked two days after a storm? How did that happen? I never really found out, yet all I knew was I needed to act quickly and do something to get to Toledo. It is not what you are going *through*, it is where you are going *to*. I was in my first year, with a new supervisor, and I was *not* going to miss a game because I couldn't get there.

Side note: I had multiple tickets on my car when I returned, totaling hundreds of dollars in fines. #notcool. I was able to appeal them and got it knocked down to just two! Good news: the LeatherMan was safe in the snow, and after some digging for a few minutes, I got it back!

7. Andrew, sorry about your Dad.

Early November 2008, exhibition game, George Mason University, Fairfax, Virginia

My Dad died on November 2, 2008. We had just completed our third New York City marathon with my brother Paul, and my Dad had a heart attack when he arrived home. He was just 66, and we were all devastated. I am blessed that we have a video of that special day with him that you can view here:

I was mentally exhausted after my Dad's passing and services and not really ready to get back on the court. I had an exhibition game the next week at George Mason University (GMU). On the four-hour drive down to the game, I mentally prepared not to think about my Dad, focus on the game, and know that he would want me to do an outstanding job.

I was ready. Just a few minutes to go before the game, and I was ready. Not thinking about Dad, but thinking about running like a gazelle, making perfect calls, having excellent mechanics. As the warm-up clock was down to the last couple of minutes, the refs walked over to shake hands with the coaches, visitors first, and then the home team (GMU). *Have a good game*, I repeated over and over, as I had done a few hundred times.

I went to the last coach on the GMU sideline, Chris Caputo, a native New Yorker. Chris grabbed my hand, held on longer, and said, "Andrew, I am so sorry about your Dad." What? How did he know that? He actually cared enough to say something. It hit me like a ton of bricks. My knees buckled because I was not ready for that. I fought back tears, graciously said, "Thank you," and kept moving.

Coach Caputo's take:

By Chris Caputo. Chris Caputo is currently the Associate Head Coach at University of Miami. He has been the longtime assistant to Jim Larranaga at Miami and previously at George Mason University. I always appreciated Chris' professionalism and coaching on the sidelines.

A lot of times, in coaching, you get to know the referees. You see them year after year, every couple weeks. You try to build up a good rapport in this high-stakes, tense environment. I think, a lot of times it's easy to forget the humanity involved.

Going back to that time, I believe Ron Bertovich, the associate commissioner of the CAA (Colonial Athletic Association), told me about Andrew's father. Learning not just that he passed away, but the unusual and sudden way in which it happened, I could only imagine what Andrew was going through at that time.

The gesture was how I was raised and how my coaches, I think, would've handled a situation like that and how Coach Larranaga would've handled a situation like that. I don't think it's anything

I deserve any sort of credit for. After years and years of getting to know people, when they lose a loved one, you want to at least make some sort of gesture of condolence.

As Dean Smith said, "You should never be proud of doing the right thing. You should just do the right thing."

Now that I know Andrew was trying to put it out of his mind that day, maybe I brought it up at the wrong time. But I feel like you try to treat people how you want to be treated. I think it was just a situation where, from a humanity standpoint, you want people to know our lives transcend whatever we're doing that day for work.

Leadership Takeaway: I write many times in this book that *It's the little things.* This was a tiny act of compassion that left a huge impression on me. At that moment, when Coach Caputo said that to me, it meant so much. We were about to go into this intense game together, and for that short moment, he showed empathy, care, and genuine sympathy for my loss. I was always a fan of Chris after that moment, and still root for him today at the University of Miami.

Acknowledge people's losses in their lives, even if they are strangers. Little things can mean big things to others.

8. We're not gonna take any s%$# tonight!

Thanksgiving eve, 2003, Curtis HS vs St. Peter's HS, College of Staten Island (NY).

The big game. My first "big game." This was the night before Thanksgiving where alumni, friends, and HS basketball fans gathered in the gym and around the TV to watch this big rivalry. My first TV game, and the first time I got to work with the legend Nick Gaetani. Nick looked like an actor right out of the movie *Goodfellas* or the hit series, *The Sopranos*. His accent was the thickest you've ever heard, he was tough as nails, and he was just the best guy. The refs loved him, yet a lot of others, including coaches, feared him, because they knew he wasn't going to take any s%$#.

I was a bit nervous because of all the firsts listed above, but I wanted to act cool because I was with Nick, the legend—"The Godfather," as they called him. When I am nervous, I walk fast, and my ears turn red. Both happened as we left the locker room together to walk to the court. Someone was holding the doors to the court open for us, and I walked in first. The bleachers were to my left, and I was moving toward the court. I felt a strong pull on my shoulder from behind, and someone pulled me under the bleachers.

Nick had a crazed look in his eye. He stuck his boney finger in my face inches from my nose, and, with his teeth clenched, almost in a snarl, he grunted, *"We're not gonna take any S%$# tonight!"* Then he slapped me hard right across the face!!! Yes, *slapped*.

What the? I was stunned, not even able to absorb what was happening. He spun me around, pushed from behind, and yelled, "Now get out there and do a great job!"

Leadership Takeaway: Leadership can take on many forms, sizes, shapes, and sounds. This story sounds made up, but I assure you, it is not. Any refs from NYC who are reading this who knew Nick know that this is how he was. I couldn't believe that had just occurred, as I stood on the court, embarrassed and beet red.

What happened over the next few minutes was even better. I felt calm. He'd slapped the nervousness right outta me. I wasn't thinking about the game, the TV, the bright lights, etc.—I was thinking that this crazy old Italian just slapped me!

He knew I was nervous. He knew I was tight and took the steps to snap me outta of it. Can you slap people in today's world? No, but back then, it was appropriate at that moment, and more importantly, it worked. I had a great game, Nick was proud of me, and hugged and kissed me like a real Italian afterwards. I proved to him that I was tough enough to rebound from the slap and perform like he knew I could.

In your leadership, don't be afraid to step out of the norm sometimes—be different, be bold. Again, I caution you: don't hit people, but don't be afraid to make your mark on others with your mentorship, leadership, and impact. Nick sure did!

9. Stand tall.

December 2, 2006, Seton Hall vs. St. Mary's (California), The Meadowlands, East Rutherford, New Jersey.

As I moved on in my officiating career, I began to work in bigger venues and arenas. New season, next year, bigger arena. This was exhilarating but also challenging. If you were in an average HS gym, you did not have to project too much of yourself: your signals, your whistle, your actions. You just called the game, worked hard, and kept moving.

As I moved to these larger spaces, I began to experience the need to expand: expand my energy, the strength of my whistle, my voice, etc. My first big jump was a game at the Meadowlands, the old New Jersey Nets arena west of New York City.

Firsts

It was a cavernous, older arena and, in 1996, the last arena to host a Final Four not played in a football dome. I felt like a miniature person in the space, and I needed to expand my presence. I began to stand a little taller, be a little bigger. I focused on my body language, making sure I was standing up tall, keeping my shoulders back, and showing strength in my actions. Not reaching further, not trying harder—just focusing on being a bit taller. This gave me more confidence in the space to know that my actions would be received not only by those right in front of me, but those seated in the upper rows and outer spaces.

Leadership Takeaway: This slight adjustment of *standing taller* helped me to move forward not only in my officiating career but also as a leader. When I landed in the Carrier Dome in Syracuse, New York (Syracuse basketball plays their home games in the indoor football arena), I was able to project myself better, feel more adequate, and be more confident. It is an amazing gigantic space, and you could get lost in it.

As I grew as a leader in schools, I transitioned out of the classroom and began speaking in bigger spaces: auditoriums, cafeterias, etc. As a keynote speaker and presenter, I moved from conference rooms to giant meeting spaces and arenas. You have to stand tall. You have to project confidence and your voice. It can be more challenging to reach your audience, so I challenge you to #StandTall in whatever space you are working. It will serve you well in the moment and in your future.

2
POINTS OF LEADERSHIP

Before you are a leader, success is all about growing yourself. When you become a leader, success is about growing others.
—Jack Welch

10. Never miss a chance to let them see you shine.

From my friend, mentor, and former supervisor, John Clougherty. John said this many times over the years, in meetings and conversations. It was his expectation of his officials, young or veteran. At first, I thought it was related to being cocky. It didn't fit with John as a man and leader, because he was so humble.

The more he shared examples about it, I started to get it, and the longer I was around great officials, I began to see it and absorb it. From the moment we stepped out of the car, never miss an opportunity to let them see you shine...let them see the reason why you were there, chosen to ref that game.

- *A warm smile and greeting to the security on the way in.*
- *Ask the person walking you to the locker room about themselves and their goings-on. Take an interest in them.*
- *Pre-game routine: stretch, hydrate, meditate, warm up, take care of your equipment, etc.*
- *Review all the pertinent details of the game, the points of emphasis, what we would focus on as a crew.*
- *Stand tall out on the court. Look the part: confident, upbeat, and focused.*

These are just five examples of letting your professionalism shine through—without ever even blowing the whistle. Obviously, you have to hustle, get the calls right, know the rules, etc. and do an awesome job in the game. Yet it is these other techniques, strategies, and actions that separate the good from the great. Many examples of professionalism have nothing to do with basketball or refereeing.

Leadership Takeaway: There are so many ways to shine, regardless of your work. You are in your position for a reason. Why? There are too many reasons to count, so don't be afraid to shine in your role. You are *not* showing off or trying too hard; you're showing confidence, taking a genuine interest in the lives of others, and enjoying the journey. Lead your life and work tasks with energy, spirit, and the goal of doing an amazing job. Life is a series of tryouts, so keep shining and keep succeeding whatever the situation. Remember—someone is always watching. So, *shine!*

11. Be the best team on the court.

By Ron Bertovich, Commissioner, Atlantic 10 Conference, 1986–94, Commissioner, Mid-Con Conference, 2003–05, Deputy Commissioner for Basketball, Colonial Athletic Association, 2005–17. Ron is a great friend to the officials, loves the game of college basketball, and was a great leader in college sports.

As a senior member of the leadership team of an NCAA Division I conference, it is absolutely imperative to remain as neutral as possible when dealing with the member institutions. Trust me—people notice (and often remind you) when favoritism is perceived.

With oversight of men's basketball as my top priority, I would attend 90–100 games per season, with a vast majority of those games pitting two conference teams against each other. Intraconference games are always of higher importance as the results and final standings dictate each team's seeding in the postseason conference tournament and a potential ticket to the NCAA Tournament.

Upon arrival at these games, I always would visit with staff members from both teams, the television broadcast team, and local media in attendance. However, it was the 30-second pregame handshake with each game official that, to me, was the most important. I can guarantee you that I was the *only* person in the arena cheering for the three men in striped shirts. My life would always be a lot less stressful if the officials did their job with minimal consternation. I stressed communication with players and coaches and consistency in their calls. Whether visiting with a 30-year veteran or a rookie working his first conference game, I ended each greeting with...*We need to be the best team on the court.* I truly believe the officials were somewhat comforted by the support and often thanked me for my comments.

I should also add that during the under-4:00 minutes media timeout of the second half of each game, I would say a silent prayer: *Get it right, stripes.* If an official came near my courtside seat, I would always encourage them to "Finish Strong." Again, I am most certain that my comments were much more positive than the choice words the officials received from coaches and fans. While I was often "accused" of over-support of game officials, I truly feel the officials appreciated me recognizing the difficulties of their job.

Leadership Takeaway: Everyone wants to, and needs to, be appreciated. Show others that you care, and encourage them to be successful, both individually and collectively. If you make a mistake, "own" it, learn from it, and move on. Enhancing communication and trust will always help all entities to resolve issues when they arise.

Ron Bertovich

---

12. In it for the long haul.

The big-timers grabbed my ear early in my career and shared some of the tricks of the trade—tips and strategies to keep healthy and take care of yourself not just for this game, but for the long haul. I would see them riding the bike, warming up before the game, in the training room, getting taped, stretching, and more. Afterward, ice, stretching, compression pants, etc. I always quickly showered, jumped in the car, and was on my way.

A veteran and I had breakfast one morning before the game. He asked, "Kid, you want to do this a long time?" I, of course, eagerly said, "Yes." He continued, "Don't wait until you get hurt to start doing the things that will keep you going. Invest in great shoes, get a pair of custom orthotics, stretch each game, heat and ice each game. Invest the time and energy in yourself. If you don't take care of your body, who will?"

Leadership Takeaway: This is a marathon, not a sprint. Whatever your business, leadership role, or success journey, do the things that will continue to help you be successful. The "overnight" success stories have been grinding for years. How can you keep going until you "make it"? You gotta take care of yourself. You have to invest time, money, and the best practices of self-care on yourself. I started to tell people: These feet make me a lot of money and keep me moving. I invested in great shoes, orthotics, pedicures, podiatrists, and more. I bought the best clothes, gear, equipment, etc. If you want to be in it for the long haul, invest in yourself, and do the little things each day to take care of yourself. I am so grateful to those vets who showed me the way and offered health and longevity tips. They worked for me then and still serve me well today.

13. It's time.

By Roger Ayers. Roger is a longtime, highly successful men's basketball official. He has been at the top of the game for what seems like forever. Final Fours, Championship games, the big games, and as he writes below, a leader and mentor for many, including me. He also has the best hair in the game. I thank Roger for his leadership and willingness to help others along the way.

As an NCAA Men's Basketball Official for more than 20 years, I am often asked what some of my most memorable moments have been along this journey. Most are surprised at my answer. Yes, I talk about the big games, the Final Fours, my first Duke/UNC game, the great players I have been honored to officiate, along with some Hall of Fame coaches. But the moment I realized I had to become a *leader* actually happened off the court.

In 2006, I received a phone call from my then-Supervisor of Officials in the ACC, John Clougherty, and I will never forget what he said to me...*It's time.* I wasn't sure what he meant at the time. He went on to explain to me that he needed me to step out of my comfort zone as an ACC Official and become an ACC Leader. From that phone call on, I have never looked back. *What does it mean to be a leader?* I thought that night. I needed to now lead my crews each night on and off the floor. A big responsibility for sure in one of the highest-profile leagues in the country, but I was ready. To be a leader means that you have to have the trust and support of those who follow you. Each game I work, I want my crew to look at me not only as a leader but as a fellow official, colleague, and friend who will never let them down or leave them hanging in an ugly situation.

Officiating, as in life, is hard, and each game brings a different set of circumstances—but a true leader is ready to handle whatever situation arises. I take it as a challenge to be not only a great official but a great leader to my fellow officials. I want them to know that I've got their back and that nothing will happen to them on my watch.

Leadership Takeaway: Many people want to be a leader, but to do that, one must step out of their comfort zone, go to the front of the line, and do the things that great leaders do—that is, lead and not follow. Leaders take chances and take risks. Yes, some will make mistakes and fail, but the great leaders get back into the game and start leading again. It is easy to stay in the background and be a follower, but it takes a special person to step up and accept the challenge to lead others. I am so grateful I was challenged in 2006 to step up. That call not only changed my life as an official—it made me the man I am today!

Roger Ayers

14. Know something about the people/the event before you arrive.

I listened to my friend and mentor Roger Ayers on the Crown refs podcast. He dropped so much knowledge in this interview with my friend and referee Paul Diasparra. One point that stood out to me was to do some pre-work before the game. Don't just show up to the game knowing nothing about the teams, coaches, schools, etc. Do your homework. Is one team in first place in the conference standings and one team in last? Is the coach in his last year of his contract? Is the game on TV? Who are the best players on the floor?

Are all these questions related to basketball? Yes and no. Yes, *some* are about basketball, but most are about the moving parts of the game. They can help you make decisions knowing the circumstances and what is at stake.

Leadership Takeaway: Do your homework to learn as much as you can about the situations you are involved in as a leader. Ask questions, search Google, talk to people involved, and take it in. Talk with someone who has been there before. Do you need to write down notes, or can you just absorb it all from listening? Learn what you can to help guide you in your journey through the different situations you face. All information can assist you. You might not think you need it, yet you never know where the information you researched can help you. Learn what you can about the situations you are heading into. It can only help you.

Now, as a speaker who travels around the country, I like to learn about places, schools, etc. before I arrive. I traveled to little ol' Haleyville, Alabama, in the summer of '21. Did you know one of the things that Haleyville is famous for? I didn't before I traveled there, but I did discover in my research that this is where the first 911 call came from in the United States in 1968. I referenced it in my speech, told a story about it, and was able to make a deeper connection with my audience because I did just a little digging and research prior to taking the stage. It is well worth your time.

15. The fax.

Wednesday, March 19, 2008: First round NIT game, Cleveland State at Dayton, Dayton, Ohio

It's the little things we remember, isn't it? It was my first NIT game, and I was a bit nervous. After working out at the hotel, I was meditating in the room, mentally preparing for the game, and the phone rang. I was startled and took the call. The front desk informed me that I'd received a fax. A fax? What? I thought I was coming off the game or something like that...bad news from the NCAA?

I popped down to the front desk and was pleasantly surprised to receive a handwritten note from my best friend, Dr. Francis Celis. Francis and I have been the closest of friends since grade school, and he continues to be an amazing friend today. He sent me a note offering congratulations, words of encouragement to enjoy the moment on the big stage, and that he was proud of me and would be watching.

I welled up reading it. It was so thoughtful and kind of him to acknowledge this moment for me in my life. I fondly remember the note and how I felt receiving it. Thanks, Fran!

Francis's take:

By Francis Celis. Francis is a cardiologist and my lifelong friend. He is a native New Yorker, a first-generation proud Filipino, husband, father, and sports fan. He moved his family to Corvallis, Oregon, serving that medical community.

If you're lucky enough to meet your best friend in first grade, you get to share life's major events. Not just the obvious milestones like weddings, children's births, graduations, but smaller events and triumphs that few others outside the immediate family might be privy to. And so it was that night when I realized Andrew would be amping up for one of the biggest professional nights of his life. I knew that he could use a few kind words of encouragement and be reminded to just enjoy the moment. As part of Andrew's small circle who knew about this, I felt honored to share one of the pinnacles of his college refereeing career. In all honesty, I didn't remember writing that fax until Andrew mentioned it to me. But it just goes to show that small, forgotten gestures on your part may impact those you love for a lifetime.

Dr. Francis Celis

Leadership Takeaway: Acknowledge the accomplishments of those around you, the closest, and even in outer circles. People are working hard and doing the best they can (in most cases). For a little of your time, a kind act of reaching out goes a long way. It shows the character and respect Francis has for me and our

friendship. This act of friendship made me think about my actions toward others and inspired me to reach out more to acknowledge the victories and successes of those around me as well console them for setbacks and failures. Connections, words of encouragement, and the handwritten note are still extremely powerful in a technology-filled world. Fast-forward thirteen years, Fall 2021. I had my first presentation in Oregon (where Francis lives), and guess who drove three hours each way to be there? That's right: Francis. #Appreciation #Friendship

16. Leadership

By John Clougherty. John, simply put, is one of the best in the business. He was an award-winning, 12-time Final Four official, and longtime supervisor of the ACC, A-10, CAA, and other leagues. He is humble, kind, and tough; he wants the best for others and his officials. He gave me an opportunity for which I am forever grateful. He is a friend and mentor, and one who did it the right way. He was elected to the North Carolina Sports Hall of Fame in 2015.

Leadership is defined not by how smart you are or how many titles you hold or the number of individual awards you've won. Leadership does not stem from power or authority, but as author John Maxwell ably puts it "leadership is influence—nothing more, nothing less."

If one agrees with Maxwell's definition, then how should one best use their influence when leading others? This can best be answered by citing two different examples and their influence on how I chose to manage.

As a longtime collegiate official and supervisor of officials for the ACC, Atlantic 10, and Colonial Athletic Association, I've had the privilege and the unique experience of working with hall-of-fame coaches, school administrators, conference commissioners, and NCAA executives. I've benefited from watching the very best use their skills and influence in leading others.

Unfortunately, I have also had the experience of working for individuals who thought leading by intimidation was the best and most effective way to get the desired results. Nothing could be further from the truth. Bullying creates a toxic culture of low morale, timidity, and fear. Fear-based leadership discourages the sharing of ideas, hinders a team approach to problem-solving, and thwarts improvement. My position, as supervisor of officials, was to encourage honest feedback, recognize mistakes, and continue to improve without fear of retribution. Officiating under the fear of punishment never works and only leads to poor performance. In sharp contrast, the best chance of realizing success is offered by individuals who encourage opposing ideas, a willingness to accept mistakes as a prerequisite of future success, and a respect for the effort.

Leadership, at its best, was demonstrated at the first round of the 2018 NCAA Men's Basketball Tournament. The University of Virginia, coached by Tony Bennett, was the overall #1 seed. The University of Maryland Baltimore Campus, coached by Ryan Odom, was the #16 seed. In the long history of the NCAA tournament, a 16 seed had *never* defeated a #1 seed—never until UMBC beat UVA 74–54. Disappointed and heartbroken, Coach Bennett could have excused himself from the postgame, justified by saying it was far more important to be with his team. Nevertheless, he showed up and delivered.

First, he congratulated UMBC and Coach Odom. "Yeah, we got our butts whipped. That was not even close. And that's first a credit to the job Ryan did. We got thoroughly outplayed." Then he talked about the historic season they (UVA) had. Most wins in the ACC, regular season and ACC tournament champions, and the #1 seed in the NCAA Tournament. "I told our guys, 'You know, this is life—it can't define you. You enjoyed the good times, and you've got to be able to take the bad times.'"

When Andrew asked if I would write an excerpt on leadership for his newest book, I accepted without pause. Through his writings, clinics, seminars, and podcasts, Andrew has effectively integrated a proven system for leadership development. Andrew believes helping others become better leaders, regardless of one's profession, helps us all.

Bill Bradley states in his memoir, "Leadership is what unlocks people's potential and challenges them to become better. It also sees the goodness in even the most intractable knave."

John Clougherty

17. "I'm going to hire my officials from the social."

I couldn't believe it when I heard the supervisor of the Big East Conference, Art Hyland, say these words. "I'm going to hire my officials from the social." I'm not sure if he ever did this, but I did hear him say it multiple times.

When you try out to get hired on the staff of a Division I men's officiating conference, after the games played during the day, there was usually a social at night: A time in the early evening when the officials would get together, have a few drinks, have some pizza, and certainly have some time to talk. Art Hyland used this phrase about hiring his officials at the socials as a way of saying it's all about the interactions. It's all about your relationships with others. Most times, it wasn't the calls on the court that separated the good from the great officials but rather the interactions. The relationships that officials had and the way they spoke to people. Most complaints from coaches to the supervisors did not come because of a mistake that the official made on the court, but rather something that the official said to them or how the official treated someone.

Think about this in your own line of work, your marriage, your relationships with family and friends. Like our moms taught us when we were little: It's not what you say—it's how you say it. Art Hyland was looking for how officials behaved at the social, how they spoke to one another. Were they complaining about coaches, were they complaining about the playing-court conditions, did they have a negative outlook on things, or not engaging in conversations with others? Were they on their cell phone texting in the corner, or were they looking the other officials in their eyes and being an active, engaged listener?

Leadership Takeaway: You are always being analyzed and thin-sliced. You always have an opportunity to make an impression on others. Use the gifts and talents that you have, and be somebody who people want to be around. Be someone who knows how to handle themselves in social situations. The Big East is arguably one of the best basketball conferences in the country, and its supervisor was looking to hire his officials from observing them at the social. Now, do I know if he ever did this? No, I do not, but it certainly got my attention about conducting myself appropriately at all times. Be someone people want to be around, and engage with your colleagues. You never know who's watching.

18. It's the Garden, kid.

December 20, 2008, Virginia Tech vs. Columbia, Madison Square Garden, New York City.

Thrilled to be at Madison Square Garden working with the legendary Tim Higgins. Tim was a veteran official and native New Yorker and every bit of an Irish guy from New York. The best. He could talk to anyone and knew the game and people inside and out. Tim shared many points of leadership and mentorship on that special afternoon, and I am blessed to have had that opportunity. It helped me for 20 years and beyond.

As we were about to walk out on the floor, Tim turned, looked me in the eye, and said, "This is the Garden, kid. These are great players in one of the best arenas in the country; let them play. Give them space. Don't call ticky-tack fouls here, because you will get run out of town. Let the players play, and give them the space they deserve. No one wants to see you referee—they want to see great basketball in the best city in the country. He asked firmly, "Got it?" and I nodded "Yes."

His words were ringing in my head while we supervised the players out on the court before the game began. I made a mental note to hold the whistle a little bit more and not blow unless I was 100% sure. Sure enough, a few minutes in the game, there was a play coming toward me while I was the official under the basket.

There was a slight bump at the foul-line area as the play was going toward the hoop. My initial instinct was to call foul.

Tim's words rang in my ears, eyes, and heart about space and to let the talent show through the game. As my brain registered that what just happened was probably a foul, I did *not* blow the whistle and did not react. I paused, the player continued to dribble, went around the defender, and laid the ball up and into the hoop. As the ball was coming through the hoop, I told myself: *That was it! That's what Tim was talking about. That was a play that I usually would have called a foul but held the whistle.* I did it, and I was proud of myself.

I looked up quickly and saw Tim staring at me; he gave me a nod and a wink. I froze: not only did I get the no-call right, but Tim saw that I did not blow the whistle! He acknowledged to me that that was the kind of play he was talking about. I was thrilled. I felt proud and accomplished at that moment and had a great rest of the game. Tim never said anything further about the play, but I knew that was what he was talking about, and I nailed it! #givethemspace

Leadership takeaway: Give the space that is needed in the right situations. What Tim was describing was college athletes at their best. Regardless of your work or role, give people the space and time to do their jobs the best they can. When direction or correction is needed, it's our job as leaders to provide that, but we don't want to overdo it or do too much of it. That hurts the game; that hurts people's growth and their belief in you as a leader. Remember: *This is the Garden, kid—let them play.*

19. Impact

By John Adams. John was the National Coordinator of Men's Basketball Officiating for the NCAA for eight years, from 2007 to 2015. He brought many facets of leadership to this role, including improvements in consistency, transparency, and technology. He served as a Coordinator of Officials for many years.

Leadership is in all we do. So much of my work revolved around leadership. Here are a few thoughts that have helped me over the years regarding leadership:

- *1. Look someone in the eye, and tell them the truth. Answer any questions honestly.*
- *2. Don't ask someone you lead to do something you wouldn't do yourself.*
- *3. The best leaders are able to "look around the corner," i.e., see a bit into the future.*
- *4. Keep it personal, yet professional.*

As a leader, your words have an impact. I can't tell you how many times I hear from officials I've met at a camp, clinic, etc. who tell me, "What you said to me had a big impact on how I approach the game and officiate it." Rarely do I remember those interactions, but it goes to the idea of always telling the truth.

My eight years as the National Coordinator of Officials at the NCAA were marked mostly by inter-league squabbles and strong disagreement about the rules. One league thought freedom of movement was a great concept, and another league hated it. I knew it was a direction that we needed to head in, because the scoring of points was so abysmal. This concept (freedom of movement) actually didn't increase the number of fouls, but it changed the type of fouls we called. A simple thought for me: If you allowed the better players to play without getting knocked around, then the better players would play better and raise the quality and scoring of the game.

Regarding some things I would do differently, two decisions come to mind. I didn't treat two veteran officials with the respect they deserved. First: I thought a championship official from the previous year was past his prime. I assigned him to a play-in game in the first round, and that was it. I should have given him two games in the first rounds and see what happened. I regret this decision and told the official a couple of years later. Second: I dropped a respected official who had worked the tournament for many years without giving him a heads-up. He deserved at least that from me, and I failed in this situation.

Leadership Takeaway: In my time at the helm, I tried to make the overall experience of college officiating better. I wasn't perfect but tried my best. We created fair and transparent evaluations by people I trusted. I looked to minimize inconsistencies in the leadership of our leaders, help shape the rules so that they made officiating sense, and improve communication by all: TV and media announcers, our training of officials, coordinators to officials, official to coaches, etc.

Communication, honesty, doing the right work, and transparency were all part of the leadership plan I wanted to bring to the NCAA and officiating during my time. It is a great game, and it was an honor to serve as the leader for those eight years. I hope my impact helped those I served. I wish my guys and the NCAA the best in their journey.

John Adams

---

20. Same play the same way.

I learned this concept of leadership while attending the annual NCAA officiating meetings in the fall of each year. John Adams (excerpt above), the National Coordinator of officials, would visit four different regions of the country: Northeast, West, South, and Midwest and share about the points of emphasis for the upcoming year, as well as this concept: Calling the same play, the same way. He stated: whether it is UCLA vs. Oregon or Georgetown vs. St. John's, that we should call similar plays in similar ways, in accordance with the rules. He would show examples of almost identical plays that were called differently in different parts of the country. And I heard all the arguments: the score of the game, the time of the game, etc. The point was: With the increasing amount of TV exposure and replays, we needed to be consistent for the good of the game.

Leadership Takeaway: It is important in our roles as leaders that we use this leadership tool often: The same play, the same way. In this case, scenarios or situations, not necessarily plays. Not all the time, because I also believe in the concept of you treating everyone fairly, not the same. To be consistent in your practices, this concept helps: same scenario, similar outcome. We do see many of the same types of situations in our journey of leadership and decision-making. This is the power of experience. Remembering and recalling what you did in certain situations will help guide you in the next. Same play, the same way.

21. Be the ref everyone wants to work with.

I heard Roger Ayers say this on the #CrownRefs podcast. I love it, and it just sounds so simple. Why don't we work on this more? Whether as an official or in your workplace, we tend to focus too much on ourselves, our own work, and our own issues. Instead, if we make it about helping others, trying to do good for those we work with, and being a good partner or colleague, I believe that, in turn, we will be boosting our own performance. When you make yourself available, approachable, and helpful to others, you:

- *Model the behavior that others want to be around.*
- *Offer much-needed support and guidance.*
- *Focus on others.*
- *Expand your reach and value.*
- *Have a positive impact on those in your circles.*

Leadership Takeaway: Roger is that ref that others want to work with, and after experiencing working with him, I wanted that not only in my officiating world but in my personal and professional life as well. I wanted to be the Principal everyone wants to work with, be the father that kids want to have, and the husband that my wife wants. Keep in mind, not with the goal of having people like you, but with the goal that you can help and inspire others. Roger was always gracious, humble, inclusive, and more in his interactions. I loved when he'd make comments after a really difficult game like: "We fooled 'em again" or "My partners' backs must hurt from carrying me all game!" Be the leader that others want to work with.

22. You can't do it all by yourself.

by Dr. Harold Abraham, Principal/Supervisor of Special Education. Played college hoops at Montclair State University (New Jersey) from 2008 to 2011. He also works as a Professor in the Educational Leadership program at Montclair State University.

Whether you're an athlete, referee, school administrator, or business tycoon, it is undeniable that there are many lessons that translate from the hardwood to the workplace and life in general. As a school administrator for the past seven years, I have found myself on many occasions reflecting on teachings from my time on the court.

As a student-athlete on the Men's Basketball team at Montclair State University I learned a lot. I learned a lot about myself, my teammates, and effective leadership. People always joked that our coaching staff, led by the legendary Ted Fiore, was nearly as large as our roster. This staff included Bill Brooks (Mayor of Rutherford), Ed Ward (Analytics Expert), Artie Pasqualie (Actor on *The Sopranos*), Ben Candelino (New Jersey Nets Scout), Will Bishop (Player Development), Gian Paul Gonzalez (Motivational Speaker), and Darren Rowe (Former Overseas Standout). Yes—we had eight coaches in total.

After a Holiday Classic Tournament in Scranton, Pennsylvania, I remember asking Coach Fiore a question about our coaching staff. I asked him, "Why do we have so many coaches?" His response to me was one that I will never forget and one that has helped shape my leadership style ever since. He said, "Because I'm pretty damn smart and even better looking, but I'm not crazy enough to think that I know it all." He went on to explain how each and every member of his staff brought something unique to the table. He was 100% right. Each of them were talented in their own specific domain. The same applied to our team of student-athletes. We were never a single-dominant-player type of team. Instead we had a group of very talented players who worked hard and worked together. Collectively this mindset helped make us the powerhouse that we were.

Leadership Takeaway: Many novice leaders make the mistake of trying to do it all by themselves. This intrinsically comes from a good place—wanting to do what's best for their organization. However, it's simply not a best practice. In order to obtain maximum success, you have to identify the talents of the people around you and motivate them to work toward a common goal. As a school administrator, I know that I will be only as good as my staff allows me to be. Therefore, I create committees, design programming, and work collaboratively with them. In return, they enjoy coming to work, produce high-quality work, and the students in my school reap the benefits.

Dr. Harold Abraham

23. Stay in your area.

You could say I am outspoken, loud, and more. This leadership concept of *staying in your area* has helped me rein myself in and keep focused on my job and my goals. As an official, there are clearly defined areas on the floor that a certain official, depending where the ball is, is supposed to call. When I learned this through the trainings, it helped simplify and dial things in for me. The court can be huge, but if I can narrow my focus and keep my attention on a smaller area, I can increase my chances of being right in that area because it has my full attention.

A few thoughts come into play here:

- *You have to trust that the people in the other areas are doing their job.*
- *Go out of your area only if it is a major incident that needs to be addressed.*
- *Keep your eyes on the prize…that is, what's in front of you.*

Leadership Takeaway: I believe that leaders should have an expansive reach. I believe that we can add greater value in certain areas, like this book, for example: I know it can reach beyond the world of officiating into many areas of leadership. Yet *know when to stay in your lane, in your area.* I work in schools at the secondary level. I know this world very well. I don't go down to the elementary school and start telling them what to do. When my wife's cooking, and I peek over her shoulder and start to think about offering advice (I have learned from the Jedi master), I stop myself because I know that is not my area at that moment. If the kitchen was on fire, yes, by all means, jump out of your area to help, but if she is cooking, and it's going fine, leave it alone. Know space and time, learn to stay in your area, and know when to come out.

3
FAILURE TO SUCCESS

Failure is not the opposite of success. It is part of success.

24. Who is the foul on?

January 30, 2016, Delaware at Towson, Towson, Maryland

On this particular Saturday, I was officiating a game between Delaware and Towson University. Delaware was winless in the league and scratching for a win. It was a hard-fought contest, tooth and nail, all the way to the end. Late in the game, #23 committed his fifth foul for Towson near the foul-line area. My partner emphatically waved off the foul, turned his back to the play, and waved his arms signaling a no-basket call. My partner checked the scene again and intended to report the fifth and final foul on

#23, which would have removed him from the game. As he turned around, again to check the scene and report the foul on #23, #33 was standing there instead. #23 had run toward his bench in utter disappointment, knowing it was his fifth foul. My partner reported the foul on #33. The other ref and I were supervising the other players and waiting for play to continue when Delaware questioned, "Who was the foul on?" I asked my partner who the foul was on, and he said "#33." Delaware huddled, spoke with one another and then once again said to me, "Are you sure? Who's the foul on?" Again, more emphatically, I asked my partner who the foul was on, and he responded once more, "#33."

One of the most important components of officiating is to trust your partner. After asking him twice, I was confident in his answer, and we moved on. As the game drew to a close, #23 for Towson hit a three-pointer at the buzzer to tie the game (see photo—yes,

that's me and my bald spot watching) and subsequently scored all seven points for Towson in overtime, earning them a close win. Delaware went home still winless.

Maybe about a half-hour into my drive home after the game, I received a phone call from my supervisor asking about the play. I shared what happened, recounting that my partner confidently answered "#33" when I asked who the foul was on. My supervisor asked me if I checked the monitor at that moment, which I was allowed to do by rule, to confirm who had committed a foul or who had been fouled. He told me he was sending me a video clip to review. I pulled into the nearest rest area and became sick to my stomach as I meticulously reviewed the clip. As my partner turned his back to wave off the basket, #23 knew he'd committed the foul and ran in anger out of the field of vision of my partner, leaving #33 standing there. That's who he incorrectly called the foul on, #33.

As the head referee in the game, it was within the rules to confirm what happened on the floor. I should have checked the monitor. If there was doubt on the play on behalf of one of the teams, it was my responsibility to use the rules to do what is right for the game, and, in this scenario, reviewing the replay monitor was appropriate and within the rules to do so.

Leadership Takeaway: Use the rules in the real world to help you as much as you can in a variety of challenging situations that arise. You can never go wrong when you answer someone with "by rule or by law." When you look back at what you did in that situation, using the rules to your advantage will help you not only make the right call but also keep you safe in so many aspects of your life, especially your job. In this instance, I should have used all the tools available to me to make sure I got it right!

25. Not straight at all.

Sometimes the great ones just make it look easy. Like they never struggled, like they never made a mistake. They are just smooth and graceful, and they were born like that. But we all know that's not true. When people have made it to the top of their game, they have been through the battles, the failures, the mistakes, and then some. It just *looks* easy.

Yet we know it's not. It's hard work. It's messy. It is persistence. It is not giving up. It is failing and keep going. It is all of that and then some.

I love the picture below. People think it is easy…straight, smooth sailing. It is most definitely challenging and mixed up. Look back and forth between the two pictures. Think of the journey you are on, where you have fallen short, made a mistake, or got tangled up, like in the picture.

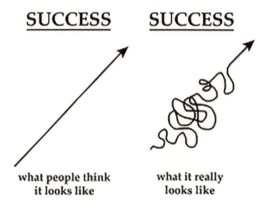

Leadership Takeaway: How did you keep moving forward, keep going? How did you succeed? There is no magic formula other than hard work, persistence, and the right attitude. It's the "I'm not going to give up or quit" attitude that will propel you forward. As you read this book, as you move in your journey, use this picture as motivation to keep going and know that it is not always easy. It is/will be a struggle. As I write this book, I face challenges that I did not have with my previous books because I am busier now because of those books, so scheduling the time to write, be with family, speaking, etc. is all a greater challenge. Keep rolling and keep working through all that you have in front of you. The image reminds me of the 5SWs. These points help move me forward, and they remind me that it is not always going to work out:

- *S*ometimes it *W*ill.
- *S*ometimes it *W*on't.
- *S*o *W*hat?
- *S*omeone's *W*aiting.
- *S*o *S*tick *W*ith it.

26. You're not even on the list.

July 2006, Tryout camp for ACC and CAA leagues, Indianapolis, Indiana.

I was trying out for the Colonial Athletic Association men's basketball officiating roster. The new supervisor of officials was John Clougherty (thanks to John for writing an awesome contribution earlier in the book), the recently retired Hall of Fame CBB (college basketball) official. I showed up at the registration table ready to go: dressed sharp, confident, and eager. The young lady at the table greeted me warmly and said, "Name, please?" I told her who I was, and she began shuffling some papers around, looking a bit flustered. Then she said, "Oh, here you are." She handed me some papers, a bag, and some other items for the camp. I glanced down at the fifty names on the paper and did not see my name. She said that they had me—I just was not on that list. She then took a sharpie, crossed out someone's name, and wrote mine. "You are number 48 now."

Hmmm, I thought. *What's up with this?* I thanked her and moved away from the registration table. I quickly processed what happened and realized that I was a "B invite." I was *not* on the original invite list and that I was just filling in for number 48. *Damn!* I thought. That stinks: they didn't even have me on this list.

I was steaming as I walked to my room. *Just a fill-in*, I thought. *I have no chance of being hired. What a waste of time and money.* I went to bed feeling defeated and without confidence.

I rose early the next morning, looked in the mirror, and told myself, "Self, let's make the best of this. You can do this!" I decided at that moment—despite what had happened—to put my best self out there—run harder than anyone, be super focused, and do a killer job! I didn't know one person there, so I just put my gear on and went out there!

After a couple of days, I felt pretty good, had received good feedback, and felt things were going in the right direction. Near the end of one of my games, I felt someone standing behind me who was not a player. John Clougherty, the supervisor, was on the court. He put his hands on my shoulders and whispered in my ear, "I don't know who you are, or where you are from, but I like you, your game, and I am going to hire you. I might even put you in the ACC! (Atlantic Coast Conference)"

Leadership Takeaway: My knees buckled at that moment. I was so proud and happy and glad I did not allow my spirits to go into the tank because my name was not on the registration form. So many times in our lives, we allow outside forces to influence things that we have 100% control over: our attitude, our effort, our focus. At that moment, I could have lost all of them, yet I just tried my best despite the list. Who cares about a piece of paper? (I sure did for those first few hours!) Do your best, and forget the rest. Control the controllables. I was so grateful to John for believing in me and giving me an opportunity. When people say, "It's politics," I disagree and share this great story.

27. So bad he ripped his pants.

February 2, 2019, Bucknell at Lafayette, Easton, Pennsylvania.

Saturday game in the Patriot League. Packed house. The coach of Bucknell was Nathan Davis. Nathan was a top young coach who was very bright and excellent at what he does.

I had officiated many of Bucknell's games and knew Nathan quite well. He also knew my second partner for the game, but he did not know the third official. Neither did I. We (the three officials) had some small talk before the game in the locker room, discussed a few important points, and then began the game. After a few minutes, I knew there was going to be a problem. The third official had made some really odd calls. Calls were made that did not fit the game and were certainly out of the norm—so much so that they should not have been called. Nathan kept his cool during the first and second calls; he protested the third call, and, after the fourth call, he jumped up so fast in protest that he ripped his pants.

His assistant coaches grabbed him and quickly gave him a warm-up to cover his pants. Nathan could not have cared less about the pants. More importantly, he wanted to get to that third official and ask him what the heck was going on. I was asking myself the same thing! I did my best to calm Nathan down and let him know that we would speak with the young official. These calls he was making were not only wrong—they were *horribly* wrong. My partner and I could not get to the third official quickly enough before the game really went to the kicker.

When we finally did get to him, we reviewed the following with him: Stay calm, call the obvious, communicate to the coach that you've jacked up a couple of those calls, and get the obvious plays. Not head turners. Calls that the grandma in the top row with the bifocals could make and get correct.

Leadership Takeaway: This young official was trying his best but was trying a little too hard. He was looking for things that weren't there. In our roles and in our jobs, we need to get the obvious plays, the obvious situations. Take care of the things that matter to people, and enforce the rules. Don't have head-turners, (decisions that you make that cause people to turn their heads vigorously and ask, *What were they thinking?*). Not every decision you make is going to be right, not everyone is going to agree with you, and that is OK! Just don't make the decisions that cause good people to rip their pants.

There are also the people who, no matter what you do, will always be unhappy. Those are the ones you should not worry about or think twice about. It's the people like Coach Nathan that you should value and respect their opinion. Coach Nathan is calm, cool, and collected and would really only say things to the officials when he thought something was out of whack. So, we knew that, when he spoke, it was important to listen, because most times he was probably right.

Whatever your line of work, especially in education, get to the obvious plays. When you make a mistake, whether with kids, parents, or school administrators, admit your mistake and move on. Do better next time. Don't exacerbate the first mistake by having a second or third head-turner. You might be replacing someone's pants if you do. #KeepRolling

---

28. Give a warning.

November 28, 2007, Wagner College at Brown University, Providence, Rhode Island.

Craig Robinson and Brown University. My first time officiating Coach Robinson at Brown. My partners had told me he could be tough, especially if he did not know you. *Don't take any s*&%,* they'd prepped me. I did not know, at the time, that he was Michelle Obama's brother, who at the time, was not the First Lady.

What I *did* know is that I wasn't going to take any s&$#.

The game started and was going fine. I had a call that went against Brown. Robinson jumped up and yelled at me. We had some dialogue, and we moved on. Next play, same actions. Third similar scenario, Robinson, yelling, and *whack*, a technical foul from me on Coach Robinson. *Whaaaaat?* He held his arms out. *Are you kidding me?!* his body language screamed. Up and down he went. He told me that *he deserved better, how could he not get a warning, that was hardly anything*, etc.

At halftime, my partners asked, "What did he do?" and we talked about his actions. The technical foul was OK, we agreed, but they advised that I should have given him a warning first. I never really had done that before, but that sounded good. Wasn't going to help me at all now.

The second half was tight the whole way. Robinson and I had minimal dialogue till the end of the game, when (*of course!*) Wagner won by one! Robinson lashed out at me that it was my fault because of the technical. As a young, inexperienced official, I felt awful.

One of the guidelines in that league back then was, if you had called a technical foul, you had to call the supervisor after the game. I was petrified. The legendary Mickey Crowley picked up the line. "What happened?" he growled. I shared that Wagner won by one point. He asked, "Any issues?" I shared about the "T" in the first half on Robinson. He asked again, "Did you warn him?" I hesitantly, timidly, said, "No." There was a long pause on the line. It felt like ten minutes. He then barked, "Always give a warning!" and hung up the phone.

Leadership Takeaway: Simply put, give a warning. It sounds too simple, but it is so true. Think how many times a cop has given you a warning instead of a ticket. A bill that was overdue with heavy fines yet with a warning first. It gives you a chance to correct the behavior without penalty.

Since that experience, I have always issued a warning: on the court, in my schools, and in my home parenting my children. Everyone appreciates it. Coaches have gone from barking and yelling at me to thanking me. Although it was never in the rules back then, I began to warn the coach. Starting with some subtle, "Coach, you gotta stop." "Coach, knock it off." "Coach!" (with a look!) Next, was a loud blast of the whistle, getting everyone's attention and boldly stating: "That is a warning on the head coach of _____. Mark it in the book." Then, I would turn and look at the coach, and clearly state: "Coach, that is your warning."

While, at that moment, they did not like it and retreated like a kid who had just been grounded, later in the game, they would thank me for not issuing a technical foul.

The point is, whatever your role, find a way to offer a warning, both formal and informal, before issuing a more serious penalty. People will respect you more for it.

---

29. The toss.

November 11, 2011, Presbyterian vs. Duke, Durham, North Carolina.

It was my first game at Duke, and I was super-pumped. Mom and my wife were on hand, and it was the game that would give Coach K, Mike Krzyzewski, Duke's legendary head coach, 902 wins, tying Coach Bob Knight on the all-time wins list. Just a little bit of a big deal.

I was working hard to be calm, to act like I had been there before, but it was a challenge. I was tight. I was trying to breathe, enjoy the moment, and focus. I was just not comfortable. We walked out on the floor, and Cameron Indoor Stadium was just electric. The place was absolutely packed, fans right on top of you, and it was loud as heck. It felt like Thanksgiving at my Grandma's home: hot, packed, loud, crazy, and people hungry; hungry for a win.

We shook hands with the coaches, went through player introductions, and we were about to take the floor. The head ref shoved the ball in my gut, and said, "Have a great game" and ran out onto the floor. OMG! Tossing the ball at Duke!

I breathed deep and envisioned a nice, high straight toss, like the ones you see on TV. Two giants were next to me as I moved into the center circle. I felt the weight of the world on my shoulders, and no matter how much I told myself, *Just relax—you got this. You are going to nail this*, etc. I just felt so tight.

The toss went up. I felt like the world stopped. Like in a movie when everything stops, but the narrator keeps talking. I heard a dull roar, like a dinosaur being shot. It wasn't booing, but it was an awful sound. I saw hands flailing around, like drunk people trying to swat a fly. Arms flying, legs kicking, cursing. What was happening? What happened? My toss went like a busted firework shooting sideways; like a helium balloon out of gas; like a bad paper airplane flying to the ground; like the best Wiffle ball curve you've seen. It might have been the worst toss in college basketball history.

Coach K leaped off the bench, bad hip and all, and screamed about the toss. He pleaded with my partner to have me do it again. My partner quickly shot back, "The next one could be worse!" He waved his arms at me in disgust. I was horrified. How could I jack up the game in seconds? On national TV? OMG.

Thank God the game took over, normal play began, and I settled in. When I finally got in front of Coach, he said, "Andrew, what the heck was that toss? You gotta do better than that!" I made light of the situation and said, "I was just seeing if you were paying attention!" and then apologized for screwing it up. He politely said, "Get the next one," and we moved on.

Leadership Takeaway: It happens. You goof. You fail. You make mistakes. I totally screwed up that toss. At that moment, I was so angry at myself. How could I have done that? Years later, I laugh at it, including now as I write this account. I wanted to perform my best in that moment when it mattered so much, and I goofed. It took a little time, but I forgave myself and had to move on. In games after that, I:

- *Asked to toss the ball.*
- *Practiced the heck out of tossing the ball.*
- *Would mentally envision tossing the ball perfectly in the future.*
- *Tossed whenever I could.*
- *Told friends that I got Coach K's attention faster than anyone in the history of his 902 wins!*

Work hard to minimize mistakes, but understand and accept that they *are* going to happen. It happened to me on the grandest stage. You gotta keep rolling and keep moving!

---

30. Next play.

Another story about Cameron Indoor Stadium and Duke University. There are a lot of special, historic venues, and this is one of them. The energy in the arena, the closeness of the fans, the storied history of Duke, etc. I was dialed in on the game and super focused to do a good job. This time, it was a scrimmage game.

As the game went on, when Duke made an error—turned the ball over, missed a pass, lost possession of the ball—the bench, along with Hall of Fame Coach Mike Krzyzewski, would yell out, *"Next play!"* They didn't publicly scold the player or pull him out of the game immediately. They coached him to get the next play right.

Next play. Because it was just a scrimmage, it wasn't as loud as a normal game, so I clearly heard the calls and urging of, "Next play!"

Leadership Takeaway: I love this concept, and I put it into my routine. Not only on the basketball court, but in my life. We make mistakes. We do try to limit them, learn from them, and not make them again, but they happen. How can you have the mental fortitude to move on and get the next play right? The next relationship, the next interaction, the customer, the next shot. Whatever it is you are working on/involved with, put your all into it. If it goes sideways and doesn't work out, get the next one right. Get the next play right. It sounds simple, and it can be. Focus on the next play, and get it right. Then, later, you can reflect on what happened and why you missed the other one, and make adjustments so that you don't make that mistake again.

31. Best write-up ever.

In tip number 24, I wrote about the play where we lost who the foul was on, and the game went sideways. It was not the error in the game that was the grave mistake, but me, as the leader, not correcting the mistake. I had a chance, as the head ref, to use the video replay to confirm who the foul was on and correct the error. I was wrong and kicked it.

This was the one and only 'letter of reprimand' I received in my officiating career. It left a profound impact on me as an official, school leader, husband, and father. While I was disappointed in myself that the error occurred on my watch, I was extremely impressed with this letter from the commissioner. It reads:

Failure to Success

> MBB ━━━━━━━━━━━━━━━ Gmail
>
> **GET IT RIGHT!**
> **2/2/16**
>
> laware at Towson M━━━
>
> 8:16 AM (44 minutes ago)
>
> SENT ON BEHALF OF COMMISSIONER ━━━━━
>
> Andrew:
>
> I appreciate your assistance in providing your report from the incident in the Delaware at Towson game on ━━━━
>
> While you did conduct a 'double check' of both the scorer's table ("Do we have a foul out?") and asking ━━━ ("who do have the foul on?"), I hope you would agree that, as the Referee in the game, there was enough doubt to use the monitor to make certain that the foul was called on the correct player (Towson #23, not Towson #33), particularly in light of the time and stage of the game.
>
> Your assignment as the game Referee is based on your experience and knowledge of your profession. The ━━━ needs and depends on our officials to focus on not only specific plays but on the totality of the game.
>
> I trust that you now realize that you missed an opportunity to remedy a situation that was certainly correctable in real time. You must use this incident as a learning tool to make certain that your focus is always where it needs

Andrew:

I appreciate your assistance in providing your report from the incident in the Delaware at Towson game on _____.

While you did conduct a "double-check" of both the scorer's table (Do we have a foul-out?) and asking _____ (Who do we have a foul on?), I hope that you would agree that, as the Referee in the game, there was enough doubt to use the monitor to make certain that the foul was called on the correct player (Towson #23, not Towson #33), particularly in light of the time and stage of the game.

Your assignment as the Referee is based on your experience and knowledge of the profession. The ____ needs and depends on our officials to focus on not only specific plays but on the totality of the game.

I trust you now realize that you missed an opportunity to remedy a situation that was certainly correctable in real time. You must use this incident as a learning tool to make sure your focus is always where it needs to be....

Leadership Takeaway: I learned so much from this incident and letter. Amazingly, I felt better after the letter, not worse. I felt supported, not punished. I thought it was extremely well written: respectful, accurate, and to the point.

As a Principal and father, I need to correct errors all the time. I need to refocus others and provide clarity. This letter helped guide me in my technique of doing this work. The commissioner, through his words in the letter of reprimand, did the following:

- *Thanked me for my report.*
- *Used words like, "I hope you would agree, and I trust you now realize." These words are supportive, not demeaning or digging. They helped me understand, not beat me down.*
- *Was extremely accurate in his description. He clearly had done his homework in talking to all involved. What he wrote is exactly what happened.*
- *Shared the expectations of focus and looking at the "totality" of the game.*
- *Urged me to use the incident as a learning tool for improvement.*

In our roles as leaders, we do need to hold people accountable for mistakes and errors. The magic is in *how* we do it. I thought this was an excellent example of leadership in action with accountability, accuracy, empathy, respect, and support.

32. If you have been doing this long enough...

If you have been doing this long enough, you are going to get your hands dirty. You are going to have a problem, a tough situation. It is never going to be perfectly clean. Know this. Understand this. One of the best in the game was Ed Corbett, another New Yorker. Maybe I am a bit biased to New Yorkers, but Eddie was one of the best! He's done a million games and has been hugely successful. Championship games, a Big East legend, and a mainstay in the NCAA tournament for almost thirty years.

In 2012, in the NCAA tourney, Eddie missed a call that went against the sixteenth-seed UNC-Asheville who had mighty Syracuse on the ropes. This was back before replay, and Eddie blew the call. The arena knew it, TV knew it, the teams knew it, and of course, Eddie knew it. It was a miss, and it happens. It happens to the best of them.

Leadership Takeaway: If it could happen to Eddie Corbett, it can happen to you. I write this anecdote with the highest regard for Eddie and what he did for me personally—as well as for college officiating. He is arguably one of the best in the game, so I write not to highlight an error, but to rather share with the leaders who are reading this book that *mistakes can happen.* If you are lucky enough to be around long enough, it is going to happen. Toughen up, brace for impact, and move on. Eddie spoke about it publicly, did interviews, and moved on. He's a class act—he didn't make up any excuses or try to explain it away. Just like he officiated, he met this head-on with grit, perseverance, and ownership.

33. I'm sorry, Coach.

March 12, 2012, Stony Brook University at Seton Hall University, Orange, New Jersey.

NIT playoff game. Stony Brook at Seton Hall. It was always good to get these assignments late in the year. It was like an affirmation of your season—that you were good enough to work in the playoffs. Additionally, Seton Hall was about one hour from my home—so, even better!

I had the opportunity to work with the great Eddie Corbett, New York referee legend. Eddie was a no-nonsense, all-business attitude and just a fantastic guy. He didn't take any s____, enforced the rules, kept his mouth shut, and did his job. I always liked his style and was excited to work with him on this night.

About a month before the game, we received another memo from the NCAA regarding enforcing sportsmanship, specifically not allowing athletes or coaches to "wave off" officials. This was viewed as a big sign of disrespect and a technical foul was to be given if a player or coach displayed this action.

The game was a tight one, and Stony Brook, the underdog, had come to play. They were "bringing it" to Seton Hall. Late in the game, Stony Brook's best player committed a foul called by Eddie Corbett. As Ed turned to report the foul, the player, in disgust, waved off Ed, and I saw it. Oh, no! What was I to do? This was Eddie Corbett. No one waves him off, and it was just in the sportsmanship memo from the NCAA. Without processing what just happened, (time, score, impact, etc.), I forcefully blew the whistle and called a technical foul.

Everyone reacted like, *"What????"* with that look on their face, like, *What the heck is going on here?* No one else even saw it! It was the player's fifth foul, and he fouled out. I knew instantly that I should *not* have called that foul. The game continued, and Stony Brook lost at the buzzer with the ball rolling around the rim and out.

After the game, we had a brief discussion about the call, and Eddie shared about calling the obvious. He asked, "Was it egregious? Did it need to be called? Did it fit the game?" I digested all of these and felt terrible about it.

In November of the next season, I had Stony Brook early in the season on the road. I knew that coaches do not forget anything, and Coach Pikiell (a class act, now coaching at Rutgers University) certainly would remember it was me that had made that awful technical foul call on his best player near the end of a tight playoff game. I decided, even though many veteran refs said I should leave it be and move on, to address Coach Pikiell and acknowledge the mistake.

I walked over before the game to shake hands with him. I let my other two partners go first so I could have a moment with him. I looked him in the eye and told him that call was a mistake and I should not have called it. He paused, processed, and thanked me. He told me it was all in the game and his player should not have "waved off" Corbett. I kept it short and kept moving.

Early in the second half, Pikiell called me over and said, "Andrew, I gotta tell you. My respect level went up even higher for you that you would acknowledge that play and apologize to me. This never has happened to me before. I really appreciate it."

Leadership Takeaways: Acknowledge when you are wrong. Own it, and get better from it. I have always subscribed to the "Admit it, fix it, and move on" mindset, and this was a perfect example. Coach Pikiell was extremely gracious—not everyone will be gracious with your mistakes. He could have easily picked a fight at that moment or given me a tongue-lashing, yet he did not. He could also have just given me the cold shoulder and still been bothered about what happened. He did not. I felt better after that interaction and was able to grow from both of those experiences. We can't take back what we've done, yet we can acknowledge our errors, apologize for them, and be committed to doing better the next time.

34. Whanua.

by Steve Donahue. Steve is the head men's basketball coach at Penn University in the Ivy League in Philadelphia, PA. I got to know Steve over the years while he coached at Cornell and at Boston College. He has been to the NCAA's three times including a run to the sweet sixteen. He is a dedicated father and husband, and a class act in his leadership role. I am very grateful to him for his excerpt.

When I returned to become the head coach at the University of Pennsylvania in 2015, I was taking over a program that, for the first time in its rich tradition, was struggling in the Ivy League. I also had a year off after I was fired at Boston College (BC). I took the year off to evaluate what I could have done better at BC. During that year, I read the book *Legacy* by James Kerr. *Legacy* is about the amazing New Zealand All-Black Rugby Team. The book takes a deep dive into the culture of the All Blacks and what makes this team so successful. For me, this book really gave me clarity in how I would rebuild Penn Basketball.

Whanua is adapted from the ancient Maori, the indigenous peoples of New Zealand. *Whanua* is your family, your friends, your team, your program. It includes physical, emotional, and spiritual dimensions. For the Whanua to move forward, everyone within it must move in the same direction. The struggles I endured at Boston College were very much caused by the lack of a cohesive group that works together for the betterment of the team. We did not always move as one. We had several players that put their own individual achievements ahead of the team. I did not foster this behavior consistently enough, and it eventually led to me being let go.

Penn also struggled with a commitment to winning and putting the team ahead of personal glory. The players had no real deep connection with each other or the coaching staff. There was no real trust between coaches and players. There was no peer-to-peer enforcement of team rules.

Whanua is the central theme of our program. Whanua means holding each other accountable to the high standards we set as a program. Players and coaches are very connected with each other. The team's success is the most important aspect of our program. I encourage the players to take ownership of the program, and we make decisions in a collaborative way. We have built trust between the players and the coaches. We recruit players that we feel will fit into our Whanau. Everyone who comes into the program must know it's all about the team. We feel this is the most critical aspect for us to win championships.

Leadership Takeaway: All in, the Whanua know the strength of Penn Basketball is that we don't care how it gets done or who gets credit for it. We will work as one unit. We will motivate and inspire each other to do better and hold each other accountable when we fall short. This attitude will allow the team to grow and move forward. That is the essence of Whanau.

Steve Donahue

4
HARD WORK

"There are no secrets to success. It is the result of preparation, hard work, and learning from failure."
—Colin Powell, U.S. Secretary of State

35. Why are you down here for scrimmages?

Fall 2010.

It was my first year in the ACC (the Atlantic Coast Conference), and I was determined to do a good job. I felt ready but was unsure of the spaces, the arenas. I had seen them only on TV, so I wanted to get comfortable in those spaces. I decided that I would make the effort to travel to some ACC schools to do some intrasquad practice games (scrimmages, where the team was playing against each other) as well as traditional scrimmages against other teams.

It was an investment of time and money (you don't get paid for intrasquad scrimmages), but I felt it was worth it for my own preparation. I selected several and made the travel plans. Some included flying down in the morning, doing an afternoon scrimmage, and flying back in the same evening. #alongday.

One particular afternoon, a veteran ACC ref asked me, "Why are you coming down here for scrimmages?" I explained that I wanted to get the experience of seeing the teams and get comfortable in the space, so that when I did come, I'd be more prepared than the first time when we were live on ESPN. He shook his head and said, "Isn't that a lot to come all the way here just for a practice game?" I said, "Yes," but I wanted to do it and thought it was best for me to be successful.

Leadership Takeaway: Sometimes, you have to go against the grain. This seemed weird to others and a waste of resources, but I felt it important to do. It prepared me for the travel, I knew where the arena was, met the coaches, etc. It all wasn't brand new the first time I went for a real game. I chose to do what was best for me, and I knew what I needed. Maybe some other people can just show up and be at their best. Not me. I like to know where I will be, what it looks like, feels like, etc. This process worked for me, and, as I reflect back, it benefited me in many ways.

How many people do you know who were late for a job interview because they got lost or went to the wrong place? How many times did the limo driver go to the wrong location? It happens. It was worth it to me to be prepared.

Hard Work

I encourage you to put yourself in the best positions possible to be at your best: resting, hydrating, preparing, and knowing the logistics of the setting you are in. Know yourself, and take care of these items.

36. Get out there and do it.

Put yourself out there. Go for the things you want in your life. I loved my time officiating, and I found that hard work paid off. I knew if I wanted to get hired at the big-time levels, I had to *get out there and do it*. Go to camps, get in shape, get the right gear, and so on. I was not going to get hired on word of mouth or because I knew so and so. I had to get on the court, get to the camp, bust my butt at the tryout, and more. Outside the reffing world, go for those interviews, go for those promotions, make that social media post, and do it!

It really bothers me when people throw out the word "politics." I know it happens sometimes, but it is too heavily leaned on as a reason for why something happened or didn't happen. *I didn't get it because...* So what? Keep rolling, and keep moving. You have to get after it if you want to get where you want to get to. Be relentless. Be passionate. Be persistent and keep working toward what you want.

Another thing that holds us back is: *I don't feel like it*. If you want to get to your goal, put yourself out there. Put your best self out there, and go for it, because if you don't, you will miss your shot. Don't blame others, politics, and so on...go for it and do what you have to do on your end to make it all work.

Leadership Takeaway: *If it is to be, it is up to me*. Simple. Go for the things you want in your life. So many times, as we grow older, we regret the things we didn't do vs. the things we did. If you want to reach your peak and your goals, you gotta go for it. Be prepared that failure will be a part of it, and when that happens, be ready to pick yourself up and keep moving...keep rolling.

37. You never know who is watching.

This experience was during my last season, 2018–2019, of refereeing, back when I had a heavy schedule of Division II and Division III games after 15+ years of officiating at the Division I level. It was a tough time for me, and I was mentally pushing to get through the games, determined to do a good job, knowing this would be my last season.

It was a Sunday afternoon game at 4:00 pm, the championship game of a three-game series of a weekend tournament. It was down in the Washington, D.C. area, so, if the game ended at 6 pm, I was in the car at 6:30 pm. I wasn't getting home until after 11 pm, which is certainly late on a Sunday. #longday

The game was very competitive, and I was working with two younger officials who might not have been ready for that type of competitive action in a championship game. Some calls were missed, and I started to grab more calls out of my area of responsibility. I had to stretch further than I normally do to handle some things in the game, which put it back in line, and, eventually, we got through it.

After the game, I was hustling to shower up and get on the road when there was a knock at the door. In came an NBA developmental league (D-league) referee scout. He wanted to speak to us about the game and review some plays. This went on for about thirty minutes or so. I had mixed feelings about this. I wanted to get on the road and get home, but I was curious about the NBA scout watching our game. He said some nice words about our performance. We shook hands, and I was off.

About two hours later in the car, the phone rang from a number I did not recognize. I decided to grab it, and it was the scout again. He wanted to speak more about my officiating with a possible opportunity to join the NBA D-league as an official. We talked about my career and where I was at in my officiating journey. He said he was going to follow up with an invitation to a D-league tryout. I was flattered and started to think about new possibilities.

Leadership Takeaway: You never know who's watching. That game was a Division III game late on a Sunday after I had refereed four days in a row at Division II and III levels. I could have just mailed it in and gone through the motions, just to get through the game. That was not in my nature. I wanted to help these young officials learn how to handle some of these difficult situations while serving the game as best I could. I did not know that the D-League scout was in the stands. You never know when your opportunity is there, and that's why you have to perform, regardless of your work, as if someone's always watching. As if.

One mental game I used to play when I refereed was I would pick out one person in the crowd and make them a supervisor of the league I wanted to get into. I would pretend it was them there to watch me officiate the game and do the best I could throughout the game, start to finish, in the hopes of being hired one day.

When you operate like that, on the edge of always trying to be at your best, you train yourself to act that way so you're constantly at your best. Act as if. Your opportunities for success and advancement are everywhere. You can't take shortcuts, take it easy, or take your foot off the pedal. Go all in. Bring your best self when it is time to show up. When you look back, will you say to yourself, "I am glad I did" or "I wish I would have"?

To end the story, after deep reflection, I turned down the tryout. I was on to writing, keynoting, speaking, coaching school leaders, and more. It was time to turn the page. I am proud of that moment, that game, to know that I did my best and that effort was recognized by the D-league scout.

38. How did you get here?

Many people would ask often: How did you get back to school so quickly? Andrew, you were in North Carolina last night at 9 p.m., and how are you at school now at 7 a.m.? Virginia Beach, Ohio? How are you here? Magic? No...simple driving. I planned out my travel very intentionally, not only because of my day job as a Principal but also because of my family. I wanted to maximize the time home with my kids.

So my magic was two parts: If the game was five or so hours away, I'd drive myself. Take half a day of school, drive to the game, drive about two to three hours after the game, and get a hotel. I would *sleep quick*, as they say, get up around 4:30 or so, and quickly get back on the road to be at school by seven, ready to go. So yes, it was a short night's sleep, but I was invigorated from the game and journey.

The second piece of magic (not really magic, just a lot of phone calls and planning) was to hire a driver. If I flew to a game, I couldn't get back to school to greet the kids and teachers in the morning because the nearest airport was almost one and a half hours away from where I lived. All of this work was the difference between one day off and one and a half, or in essence, not greeting the staff and students two days in a row.

So, many times during the week, I would hire a driver. We'd leave around seven-ish in the morning in the mini-van and arrive between 2 pm and 3 pm in the afternoon. I'd rest, answer emails, write, read, and work in the car on the way down. It was actually quite relaxing.

Boom. Gametime. Shower. In the car by 9:30 pm and back on the road. I'd lay the seats down in the back of the mini-van, lay out the pads, sleeping bag, and so on, and be sleeping by 10:30 pm. Depending on how far the game was, around 6 am, we'd be pulling into school. I'd freshen up, shave, put on my shirt and tie, and be at my desk by 6:30 a.m. #Magic! Some people knew I reffed, but most others had no idea. I started my day ready to go without most knowing I'd just driven 600 miles while sleeping in the back of the mini-van (thanks to Mrs. Marotta for letting me take the mini-van!)

Leadership Takeaway: Do what you gotta do to make it happen. I could miss one or a half-day of school, but to miss one and a half or two days in a row was tough. I busted my butt to make sure I was back for school...for the teachers, kids, and the sense of balance with the jobs. I knew I needed to be there, so I did what I had to do. Was it wear and tear on the car? Yes. Was it tough to sleep? Yes. Did I get run down? Yes. Were these long nights? Yes. In the end, it is not what you are going through, it is where you are going to. I was balancing the time and stress of the two jobs at the same time. Do what you gotta do to chase your dreams and achieve what you want in your life.

39. Invest the money and the time.

Through so many of these experiences in this book, I had neither of these: money or time. I was a young father, a busy Assistant Principal, and Principal, scrambling through it all. I learned through these experiences that, if I wanted to be successful on and off the court, I had to invest in myself—in a lot of ways. The equipment, the travel, the tryouts, the fitness...all of it went into my success, on and off the court.

If I didn't have good shoes, I could get hurt. If I didn't have a comfortable, safe hotel (Marriotts all the way!), I wouldn't sleep well. If I didn't have clean and sharp equipment, I wouldn't feel well, and so on.

The tryouts alone ranged from $200 to $600 each, not including the travel. So, if you wanted to try out for a league you were hoping to get hired in, after the travel and room-and-board expenses, you could easily be looking at $1200 to $1500. Then, there's the guilt of being away from your family, missing out on experiences with your kids, and so on. It was a lot. If you were out of shape, as they say in NYC, fuggettaboutit!

Leadership Takeaway: You gotta be in it to win it. You gotta spend money to make money. It is an investment in yourself and your future. Whether it is refereeing, writing, small business, etc., it is all an investment. That is why I dedicated this book to my wife. She believed in me, allowed me the time to be away while our kids were little, to be at these camps, tryouts, meets, etc. She invested in me. She gave me the autonomy to have an "officiating credit card" and track the expenses that I couldn't afford at the time. I couldn't have done it without her. #Grateful.

I went all in. I told myself and my wife: *If I am going to do this, let's go all-in, and I did.* Two to three camps per summer for seven to ten years. It was a mega-investment of time and money, but in the end, it worked. I had amazing experiences and financial rewards working in the ACC, Atlantic-10, Colonial, MAAC, Ivy, and Patriot leagues, and more. It was a great run, and I don't believe I would have gotten there if I had *not* made those investments. The big and the little ones: from shoes to massages, to dry cleaning, to Marriotts. They all went hand in hand in my success. To make it, you have to invest in yourself first and reap the rewards second.

---

40. Now go work 1000 games.

I was so deflated when the veteran referee told me this. 1000 games? I wanted to be hired *now*. I had a tryout camp. I was in shape, ran hard, looked good, had sharp calls…I had it all going for me, and that is what a top ref told me after camp: Now, go work 1000 games.

I digested this comment. We live in such an instant society these days. Everything is in the palm of our hands, instantly. Not those Division I contracts. Not those big games. Those are reserved. You gotta earn your way there. You have to put the time in and work your a$# to get there. If that is what you want, then I say, go for it!

Leadership Takeaway: Some catch easy, early breaks, but for most of us, it is a grind. It is a long journey of simply that: hard work. A test of persistence and continual tryout of showing up, performing, and showing up again. Rarely is there just a lucky break, but rather only the journey of hard work. So, I ask you: Are you willing to work your a$% for what you want? Whether it is in the field of officiating, book writing, leadership, management, will you keep showing up, delivering, and performing? If your answer is "Yes," I wish the best for you in your journey. If the answer is "No," find something else to do, because you are wasting your time and money.

---

41. Patience

By Gary Duda, husband, father, friend, educator, college official 20+ years, one of Philly's finest, Philadelphia, Pennsylvania.

Being a college basketball official for more than 20 years, you come to realize that success at any level requires many of the same skills needed in today's business world. Those include determination and grit, communication, collaboration, adaptation...just to name a few. But in my opinion, the skill or trait that has benefited me the most and continues to be key to my longevity and success is—no doubt—**patience.** Being able to practice patience, game in and game out, with players, coaches, partners, and, of course, fans, is crucial in how I'd like to manage the games I officiate.

I can remember, quite vividly, my second season as a young junior varsity high school official about to start in the winter of 1998. I had a very successful season the previous year and positive feedback from fellow officials and coaches seemed to suggest that I was ready for the varsity level...in the prestigious Philadelphia Catholic League...the best high school basketball league in the state. I was ready and wanted to make that jump to the "next level" after working only one season of JV basketball. So, when the schedules came out for the new season, and mine said "JV" next to each game, to say I was disappointed would be an understatement for sure.

Again, I felt ready to officiate at the varsity level. Fellow officials and coaches said I was ready to officiate at the varsity level. Joe DeMayo, supervisor of the Philadelphia Catholic League and longtime Division I referee himself, thought otherwise. No discussion. I'd be officiating another year of JV basketball…whether I liked it or not. So now, the only question that remained unanswered was would I continue to be patient and improve or become impatient and officiate that year with a negative attitude?

I chose to be positive and look for areas of improvement and work on those areas in my games…control the things that I alone can control. The following season, I was promoted to the varsity level—as all had expected—and worked some of the league's most competitive games…in my third year officiating high school basketball…not too bad. I even worked several playoff games that year, and then the "call" came from DeMayo himself. Based on his evaluation of me throughout the season, I would be officiating the league's championship game, at the Palestra, the "mecca of basketball" in the city of Philadelphia…again, in my third season as a high school official.

I remember being in the locker room getting ready with my two partners, veterans in the league, and in walked DeMayo to wish us luck. As we began to head out of the locker room and onto the court, Joe grabbed me on my shoulder and took me aside. He said the following, which I'll never forget: "I didn't promote you last year in order to prepare you for this moment…and you're ready…enjoy this moment." That game would be the first of six straight championship games I would officiate before making the jump to the college ranks.

Leadership Takeaway: Being patient, practicing patience, continues to be key to my success on the hardwood. Joe DeMayo

taught me that. All good leaders have the ability to be patient and assess issues/problems from several different perspectives. Great leaders give those they manage the time and space to grow and improve...and prepare them, when ready, to "enjoy the moment."
Gary Duda

42. Take great notes.

Conferences, workshops, meetings. Post-game, conversation with a mentor, goals. Write them down, and take great notes. Are you a visual learner, audio learner? Have ADD? Get distracted easily? Forgetful? I am certainly in the last three categories, so I forced myself to take good notes. Write them down. Each season, I had a notebook that I carried with me all season, including the conference meets. Dates, times, initiatives, goals, directives.

Hall of Fame teacher Kevin Birmingham from Port Jervis, New York (always a fan of the officials), told his students: review your notes every night. I'll offer the same advice: review your notes. What did the supervisor want to see out there? Review your notes. What is the technique I was to use in that situation? Review your notes. What was the special circumstance I was to be ready for? Review your notes. Five to ten minutes daily. This is one of those exercises that you "do a lot a little of the time" (love this success strategy). You will recall better all the tiny things you are responsible for. Use your time wisely, and make the important thing the important thing. Facebook and mindless watching of social media have dominated people's lives. I say skip it, and review your notes.

Additionally, there are so many ways to take great notes now. Voice messages, talk to text, smart notebook (see https://

andrewmarotta.com/product/rocketbook/ for the Andrew Marotta smart reusable rocketbook)

While many are still fans of the old-fashioned notebook, I have learned to love the smart notebook. As busy professionals, you can just have one smart notebook that scans to your Google drive, Evernote, etc., so you always have your notes and don't lose them.

Leadership Takeaway: Be responsible for your own learning. Engage in your meeting, conference, breakout, or wherever you are doing your work, and take great notes. They will serve you in the long run. Distractions, lack of focus, just "not feeling like it" all hold us back, so do the work. Whatever style is best for you, take and absorb the information.

---

43. Make it look easy.

The big-timers always made it look easy. They always looked so comfortable and in total control. You know what I learned after officiating college basketball for some years? That it takes time. None of the stars, whether in officiating, music, acting, writing, were stars when they started out. They worked at it. They crafted their routines. They practiced, made mistakes, persevered, and kept rolling.

I wrote about the great Nick Gaetani in tip number eight. Nick had been officiating for decades before I reffed with him. He could have reffed the game with his eyes closed and did a good job. It all takes time.

Leadership Takeaway: Keep at it. While it may feel uncomfortable while you are starting out, keep rolling. You will find yourself in challenging officiating scenarios, leadership situations, difficult business meetings—just keep working at it. Do you know how many podcasts I had done before I did my first one? None. Do you know how many books I wrote before I wrote my first one? None.

When I blew the whistle in my first freshman game in New York City so many years ago, it was so weird and so uncomfortable. I wasn't sure if I would ever get to where Nick was—where he could do it with his eyes closed, but eventually, I became comfortable. Hopefully, to someone, I made it look easy.

5
COMMUNICATION

"The art of communication is the language of leadership."
—James Humes, speechwriter

44. The beautiful brunette.

November 2009, Paradise Jam Tourney, U.S. Virgin Islands.
I always wanted to do a good job when I reffed. I had learned to train my mind to focus on the task at hand, trained my body to run when I was tired, and not react to events during the game that did not need a reaction. I also had the mindset that *Someone is always watching*, so I was used to it. So, I liked when my supervisors

were there, present at the game. I knew they were watching closely and that I would get valuable feedback from them.

In this particular game, I was in the Virgin Islands officiating the fall tournament they held each November. It was just awesome. One game a day with one day off in the gorgeous U.S. Virgin Islands. You just had to hope you didn't have the late game!!! On this day, I had the afternoon contest. My beautiful wife Jenn was in the stands, and I was loving every bit of the atmosphere, the high-level games, and certainly the setting. The Caribbean sun was beaming in through the small windows in the gym, and I couldn't wait to get to the beach. John Clougherty, my supervisor, casually walked by during a timeout and leaned in to say something to me. I was expecting him to say something like, "Watch 23's pivot foot" or "Tighten up in the post" (the area near the hoop, where traditionally the taller players matched up), yet it was nothing like that. He said, "The good-looking brunette in the front row thinks you're having a good game. You should take her out for a drink tonight!"

I laughed and covered my face. Then he went and sat with her for a few moments, laughing and talking with her, making her feel welcome and comfortable.

Leadership Takeaway: How can there be a leadership lesson in a casual comment in a game in the Virgin Islands? Leadership is everywhere and in all forms. John is an amazing guy: down-to-earth, real, hard-working, authentic, and caring. In that short moment and action, he did the following:

- *Showed he was human and cared about family.*
- *Acknowledged my wife and my relationship with her.*
- *Showed it wasn't always about basketball and officiating.*

- *Was not afraid to step out of the norm.*
- *Made me laugh, and made me relax.*

I loved it, and so did my wife. What John might not have known was that we had miscarried a baby just several months earlier. We both were in a fragile state, and she was putting on her best face, yet I know she was hurting inside. She still does today, yet she has moved on, loving me and our children unconditionally. John made me and my wife feel special in that short moment. As leaders, don't miss opportunities to do this for your people. Make it personal, real, and authentic. People will appreciate it and will respect you for it.

45. Take a deep breath, and have fun.

July 2004, 5-Star Basketball Camp, Honesdale, Pennsylvania

The great Mickey Crowley, legendary referee and supervisor from Long Island, New York, said these words to me. It was on the blacktop at the summer camp at 5-Star camp. It was 90+ degrees, and, man, it was hot. Mickey used to drive around the courts in a golf cart those days, watching officials and chatting it up with all around. He was an awesome guy with a gregarious personality.

He was watching my game one day, and I was pressing too hard, trying too hard. This has been a challenge for me my whole life, a kind of blessing and a curse. The next thing I know, the ball was about to go the other way, and I began to run. I felt two hands come from behind me, and grab my shoulders and stop me from running. It was Mickey! He said, "Are you having fun?" I answered, "Uhh, I am reffing and trying to get plays right, so yes, I guess, yes?" I answered not confidently as the play went to the other side of the court and Mickey held me in place. He continued: "Well, if you are not having fun, why are you out here?" I had no idea what to say. He repeated: "Have fun. Take a deep breath, have fun, and ref like you know how to!" With that, the players were coming back down to my end of the court. Mickey patted me on the butt, and said, "Go get 'em."

Leadership Takeaway: I did just that: Took a deep breath and loosened up a bit and tried my best to have fun. It was still stressful at times, but I remember trying to have fun in all I was doing. I breathed easier, ran lighter, and felt better. That summer, I got my first Division I contract from Mickey Crowley and the Patriot/Ivy Leagues, and I felt great. I remembered that moment for many years, especially in some of the tightest games that were just pressure-packed. A smile here, a deep breath there, and a reminder that it was just basketball helped.

This story reminds me of the great pitcher for the Brooklyn Dodgers, Sandy Koufax. When Koufax was a young pitcher in the early '60s, he threw the heat but was wild. He had tremendous velocity, yet was inaccurate in the strike zone. The story goes that one day the catcher ran out to the mound, and told Sandy, "Take a little off. You're burning a hole through my glove. Just take a little off, and I think it will help your control."

Sandy did just that and found the sweet spot of velocity and control. He went on the next few years to win the Cy Young award in 1963, 1965, and 1966. Are you pressing in certain areas of your life? Trying too hard and hurting your performance? Whichever of these lines apply to you, take 'em and use 'em: Take a deep breath, have fun, and take a little off. Maybe these will help you like they helped me and Koufax.

Communication

46. Attention to detail.

November 8, 2013, Cornell vs Syracuse, The Carrier Dome, Syracuse, New York.

It was my first trip to Syracuse to officiate at the massive, cavernous Carrier Dome. If you are not a hoops person, or just not familiar with "The Dome," Syracuse Orange plays in a football stadium, with their court tucked into the side of the huge arena. They regularly play in front of 20,000–30,000 people. Very cool and very different setup and venue.

I was calm but excited before the game. Trying to take it all in, and act "as if" I'd been there before, I worked hard to remain calm. I'd been to many gyms where managers and staff personnel came in to review the logistics of the game: TV, timeouts, award presentations, etc., so I was used to different people coming in and out of the locker room.

Syracuse was a bit different. About forty minutes before tip-off, approximately twelve people came into the room. They formed a semi-circle in front of us, and the director of operations (the ops guy!) led the conversation. He told us exactly what was going to happen and how it was to happen. Then each person went down the line introducing themselves, telling us their role for being there, and where they would be located near the court. Each spoke professionally, stood tall, and was clear in their explanations. The director asked if there were any clarifying questions, waited, and then excused his team.

Leadership Takeaway: It was the best, most clear presentation of pre-game logistics I had been a part of. Because The Dome is so big, with so many moving parts to the game—they just had *more*.

More people, more planning, more logistics, and they nailed it. At one point near the end of the game, I spoke with the ops guy to tell how impressed I was with him and his team.

When you're in charge and you have a lot on the line, be professional. Be prepared and show your audience that you are in charge through your actions and presence. The ops guy did that on this day, and the game went off without a hitch. No one noticed any difference because there were no issues. Yet, this is a massive undertaking, the running of a big-time TV college basketball event. And, yes, it is an *event*. Syracuse, along with many other schools, provided a clear path of safety, organization, and understanding so we could do our jobs correctly. They set us up for success, and, for that leadership, I am grateful.

---

47. Presence.

The importance of looking the part. After doing this for a few years, some of the referees told me that half the battle of being accepted was when you walked out onto the court. Half the trust and confidence that these coaches had in you was when you walked onto the court: looking sharp and standing tall. Make sure you looked the part: shined shoes, pressed pants, groomed hair, and so on.

I always wanted to dress nice and look good in my clothes. In most of my early years, I wore mostly hand-me-downs that were too big for me because that's what I had. I didn't know any better, and I thought that was how clothes fit (my brother is a big dude!). It's just what I was used to doing. We did not really invest a lot of time or money into my outfits.

Once I started getting competitive with this refereeing and doing it for a few years, I really got into it. I got the shiny glossy shoes as well as visited the tailor who fixed up my shirts and pants. I had to peel the stuff off me, it fit so snug and tight. I learned that that was the look.

In reading Malcolm Gladwell's book *Blink*, I learned the concept of thin slicing. He explained how people judged you in the first moments that they saw you. They would look at your body language and how you presented yourself and made quick judgments. Well, it was no different in officiating or business or sales: If you had a belly popping out or you looked a little bit disheveled or your hair was not groomed—that would go against you and hurt people's perceptions of you, especially the coach.

Leadership Takeaway: Look the part. Make sure your clothes look sharp and fit you appropriately. Stand tall. Have a great presence. Record yourself in a meeting or watch a security surveillance camera of you walking in the hallway. What do you look like? What is your body language? Are you hunched over, or do you stand tall when you are talking with others? All of these are very important for earning respect for those you work with and those you serve. It's important. Trust me. I've watched a lot of tape and been booed by 20,000 people all at once. Your body language and how you look are so important in your journey of leadership and public acceptance.

48. The game within the game.

November 12, 2012, South Alabama vs Florida State, Tallahassee, Florida.

Pumped to be working with the great Ted Valentine. If you are a ref and you are reading this book, you know TV Teddy. If you are a leader outside the basketball world and do not know Teddy, he's one of the best in the game...an icon having been through thousands of games, all in the public eye. Many leaders shy away from the difficult conversation. Not Teddy. He embraced the conversation with the coach and taught me and many others that it is *"the game within the game."* It is the super-important conversation and interaction that is so important to the success of the game and your relationship with that coach for the next forty minutes and beyond. It is the skill and precision with which you go about these conversations that make it all work. "The best ones master it," he shared, and take on the challenge with confidence, vigor, and intention.

When I started reffing, I was told to stay away from the coaches. "Get away from them," my mentors early on told me, yet the longer I did it, and the further up I went, I saw the best ones masterfully engage with the coaches when necessary. They were incredible: confident, bold, patient, great listeners, and *quick*! They were in and out and amazingly picked their spots. I proudly share the concept from Ted Valentine "the game within the game" with you.

Leadership Takeaway: Embrace the conversation. Go to the source, and use the powerful communication tools that you possess to talk with people in your organization and circles. Listen, absorb, reflect, and embrace the conversation. Too many leaders shy away from the conversation, and, sometimes, less is more. Accept the dialogue, and work through it. Learn from the experience and take on the difficult conversations. Use your skills of when and when not to respond. People want to be heard, and you are the leader to listen. You are not a doormat, but you are (even if you are not there yet) a powerful, strong listener ready for the challenge. You've got this. #embracetheconversation #thegamewithinthegame

---

49. Tell me what you saw.

One of the best lines there is. With a coach, with your spouse, your co-worker. Ask the question. You don't necessarily have to agree with the answer, nor do you even have to offer your opinion, but asking the question is your way of being an effective communicator.

So many times, conflict arises from people giving their initial opinion on a situation vs. asking the other person first what they thought, or, in the case of officiating, what they saw. It is one of the 7 Habits of Highly Effective People: seek to understand. Seek to understand what has made this coach so upset to begin with and the...wait for it, here it is, the magic word: *Listen!*

Leadership Takeaway: Why do we fight this so much? Why do we not use this tool more frequently? Is it because we are stubborn? Afraid of what we might hear? Afraid to admit when we are wrong? I wish I had started using this earlier in my marriage, educational career, and officiating career. It is the magic sauce, the calming words, and the avenue of communication that people are looking for. Ask the question and just...listen.

Sometimes, you won't even have to respond. You can offer short responses when they are completely done: *Got it, Coach. OK, Coach. I'll get a better look next time.* No *excuse*, no *but*, no *nothing*. Acknowledge what they saw, and move on. These are great communicator words: Tell me what you saw. Use them to help you in your journey on and off the court.

50. Why curse like that?

Philadelphia, Pennsylvania.

It was an early-morning practice game at the famed Palestra, the historic basketball arena in downtown Philly. Two hard-nosed Philadelphia teams going at each other in a scrimmage game: no fans, no bright lights, no media, etc. Just hoops, sweat, and Philly grit. One coach called timeout and let his team have it. He unloaded on them as I have never heard. He cussed, called them names, and berated the players. Every other word out of his mouth was a curse, an insult, and just plain awful. I almost intervened but then thought better of it...it was not my place. (Tip #23: *Stay in your area!*)

The team went on to finish the scrimmage but never really played any better. The coach screamed some more and never really got any more out of his team.

I am not sure why, but I was pretty upset afterward. Why did I care? They were big boys at the Division I level. I just had to call the plays, and it wasn't my business how that coach chose to treat his team. I thought about writing to the President of the University but never acted on it.

Leadership Takeaway: Those actions, that language, and behavior toward others have stayed with me all these years later. I vowed, at that moment, never to speak or treat others in such a way. It was so degrading and demeaning to those young men. Fear, anger, and rage: does that motivate people? Maybe in the short term, it might move people, but not in the long term. I want to have a profound, lasting impact on those I serve: one of love, trust, and respect. What kind of leader do you want to be? How do you want to treat your people? I would not want my children to be spoken to like that, so I will not do it to others. Be super-mindful about how you treat others, especially when no one is watching.

51. Reach out.

It is such a long season, almost five months long through the winter days and nights. It can be a grind sometimes, and injuries mount up. Most of my friends had an injury at some point in their careers. A tear here, a fall there, a twist, etc. Some of them were like the robotic man when they suited up, with so much padding, braces, and such.

I also made it a point to reach out and check in on them. An injury during the college basketball season can be quite isolating, so be a good leader and friend, and make that extra call, text, or stop at the house. While they say they are fine, most times the people really do appreciate it.

Leadership Takeaway: It is the little things that people remember, like the text saying, "Hey buddy...sorry you got injured. Get well soon." Yes, you are busy, with lots to do, but make the time to make these small gestures of empathy, friendship, and care. You don't have to be a traveling nurse, yet you can show amazing kindness and compassion to those in your circles: business, social, church, etc. Reach out, ask, listen, offer help. I am not the best cook for sure, but I can make a mean meatball. This is one of my favorites to do: make a tray of meatballs for a friend. People remember, so when you hear someone is injured, had a loss, got let go, or are just down in some way, reach out. Don't wait. Do it. The best ones do.

52. Good job.

I hated hearing this. I went to 100 ref camps and busted my hump all those years. Some of the evaluators would really give us the time we deserved and paid for: spoke to us, gave us real, practical feedback. Specific techniques and do's and don'ts to get hired, be successful. I couldn't stand when someone would just say, "Good job," and walk off. *Good job?* I just busted my butt for forty minutes, made eighty-seven decisions, gave out three technicals, and you just offered "Good job?" Does that mean I got hired? 'Cause if it does, I'm good then and don't need to hear from you, but otherwise, I'd like your feedback. I am trying to get hired and worked my tail off: give me some good, some bad, and some advice.

Leadership Takeaway: Be authentic and real in your feedback. Don't waste people's time with "Good job" and give no specifics: what was good, how was it good, and where they can grow. Feedback, leaders, feedback. People are craving it in a respectful, empathetic, compassionate manner, yet want to hear how they can grow and reach their goals. That is why you are in your leadership position in the first place. Not because you are above anyone, but because you can uplift them, make them better, and move them forward. Give the time and feedback your people deserve, and don't short-change people.

53. You're damn right someone is going to get hurt.

Fall, 2000ish, McKee Tech HS JV game, Staten Island, New York.

Communication

I was a young ref in my first or second season in a hot game. Packed stands, hot gym, rowdy coaches, and players. There was a scrum for the ball, with kids diving for the ball, bodies flying, and me saying to myself, "What the heck is happening?"

I must have looked like a football ref after a fumble, trying to see which team had recovered the ball as I sorted through the players, and the kid with the ball had a huge gash on his eye. Blood was pouring down his face. The coach quickly ran onto the court, attended to his player, and then began lashing out at me. "How could there not be a foul? My kid got clobbered (he probably was right)! Look at this blood!" I had no idea what to say…and I can still feel the words coming out of my mouth when I responded with, "It's a tough game out here, coach. Kids are going to get hurt."

What? Did I just say that? Why? That was awful, and my quick self-assessment of my response was accurate. The coach went through the roof: "You're damn right someone's gonna get hurt out there! You just wait and see!" He quickly called timeout and fired up his players. I am sure he told them to clobber the next guy, and that is exactly what happened in the next play. His guy creamed the kid taking a layup so hard we had to call an intentional foul for excessive contact. Not good.

Leadership Takeaway: Use your words carefully. Take a moment to process and respond. Listen. Less is more (most times). My response had incited violence and raised the level of aggressiveness in the game, not calmed it down. Also, the timing was really poor on my part. The blood was still fresh on the kid's face and literally on the coach. Probably not the best time to speak with him.

Play this out: "Coach, take care of your player, and I'll be back to talk with you shortly." This does the following:

- *Acknowledges the injury.*
- *Gives the coach some focus without over-telling him/her what to do.*
- *Gives you some time and space to think, process, and be ready to speak to the coach.*
- *Allows some time for the coach to calm down and get back into the game.*

A lot of times, the game has moved on, and they might not even want to discuss it anymore. Maybe, the injury was a slight cut that was just bleeding badly, the kid was patched up and ready to go, and it was not even an issue. Maybe later, you lead with, "Coach, I'm sorry about your kid and the injury. I missed a foul there. My bad." You might get some heat; absorb it, and move on.

Communication is very intentional and a skill that you can always work on. I am still at it today as I write this book. I replay scenarios and situations over in my head on how I can better communicate. Way back in the early 2000s, my timing was awful and my word choice even worse. I learned from it and did not do that again. #keeplearning #keepgrowing

54. Put the pasta in.

This was from another era, for sure. I finished a HS game in Brooklyn with the great Nicky Gaetani. We showered and were getting dressed, and he punched in his home number on his "new" cell phone. These were new back then, and it was an old-fashioned flip-phone that he did not have any numbers stored in. He said loudly into the phone, "Put the pasta in!"

Nicky lived just a few miles away and was going to be home in about ten minutes. I loved it. It was so old-fashioned, like out of a movie.

Leadership Takeaway: While I never called my wife and said, "Put the pasta in," I did learn to communicate with my wife and family the importance of where I was, and, most importantly, when I was coming home. My kids were very little back then when I reffed and didn't really have a concept of where I was or what I was doing. We created a weekly calendar that would show where the games were, what time, and again, most importantly, what time I would be home.

This was important to all of us. I would always pad the travel time a little bit, making sure I'd get home early, and the kids would go wild. I tried to get souvenirs and small gifts for the kids, and bring dinner home when I could to help out my wife.

Communicating where I was and when I was coming home to everyone was an extremely important part of our success as a family through the time I reffed. Whatever your business, be clear and open about your travel, and keep all parties informed.

55. Acceptance.

By Brandon Cruz, father, husband, math teacher, college official 20+ years, Long Island, New York. Brandon was one of my first friends in officiating, from way back in Honesdale, Pennsylvania, and 5-Star camp. A bright smile and a great attitude are just two of Brandon's successful traits. I am thankful for his contribution.

Having officiated now for more than 20 years, I cannot express the importance of relationships on and off the court. Positive interactions over time develop the most important piece of an official's success: acceptance. For all officials, acceptance is a critical component to the psyche and confidence on how the game is managed. Coaches indirectly feel this presence and will likely act and interact with the same recourse. As younger officials come through the pipeline, I am reminded of a situation that led me to gain some of this success.

In one of my first years in Division I, I encountered a coach who was known to be tough on officials but a decent guy off the court. I was warned by the veterans on the crew to handle my primary and converse on a limited basis until you get to know him. They said to "speak when spoken to"—a sentiment I still agree with today for less-experienced officials. As the game went on, the anger expressed by the coach with regards to my calls got progressively worse. During a timeout, I looked to my crew for a sense of how they felt about my job thus far. Both confirmed my calls and thought the coach's comments were directed at me because of my youth and inexperience. Then they had a good chuckle at my expense. At halftime, we spoke some more. After talking in the locker room and going against their wisdom, I thought it was best to confront this issue on the court early in the second period.

During a play where his guard got stripped in front of his bench and the defense started on a breakaway, his team fouled. I blew my whistle, called the foul against his team, and he started to argue as a media timeout was about to take place. I did the right thing and did not bring up the conversation that I had been rehearsing in my head since the second half had started. I allowed the comments to go, the coach took the media timeout, and I went to my position on the court. As the timeout was concluding, his huddle broke early; I walked over to make my point. Bad move.

I began with, "Coach, I feel like I am being overly judged on these plays because I'm new around here."

I know now that it was not the best time to make this comment, as if there *ever* is such a time. His team just turned it over, they're starting to lose the lead, he is on the hot seat for his job, and a new official doesn't like the way he's being treated. Imagine a red face with daggered eyes as I recall his response in a yelling tone, "I don't give a s&%$ what age you are! If you continue to miss plays, you're going to hear it from me!"

I don't know what made me do this, but it was probably the best thing I could have done...nothing. I took the loss, and I walked away licking my wounds. Officials do not like losing verbal spats with coaches. We should consider handling all situations with class and patience. Obviously, this was a learning moment, but more so a lasting one. As officials, we need to take risks. This was one of mine. We need to lose every now and then. It makes us better prepared next time.

Sometime later at a summer camp, that same coach approached me. He apologized after seeing the film and told me "we just sucked that day." He went on to say that he was surprised I didn't give him a technical foul. When he asked why, and I said, "I approached you and lost the argument." It was that hot July day in the middle of twenty AAU basketball courts with whistles coming from every direction when I took a step toward acceptance. He knows I will read the game better next time but make the same confident calls. He knows I can be approached by having an awareness of myself and the interactions on the court. It was a lucky risk that paid off in the long run.

Leadership Takeaway: Acceptance takes much more than a moment—it takes a series of moments like that. It will take years to earn, and, when you do, hopefully, you get hired again in a different role to start back at square one.

Brandon Cruz

---

56. Are we good?

Winter 2008, Old Dominion University, Norfolk, Virginia.

I was working with John Hughes, a longtime hoops official from NYC. John is a bar/restaurant owner from Queens who knew the game, knew people, and knew when to talk, and when to listen. The coach from ODU, Blaine Taylor, normally a great guy to work for, was irritated that night. He was on John consistently, yelling at him, which was out of character for Coach Taylor. John gave him a verbal warning, which Blaine rudely made further comments about, and John whacked him (slang for giving him a technical foul for misbehavior.)

John was just perfect in his execution of the technical foul. Excellent signals to the table, did not engage with the yelling Coach Taylor, and then quickly moved away from the bench area. He did not look at the coach, go near him, or speak to him.

I thought that he was done with his communication with Coach Taylor for the night. About fifteen minutes later, I see John jog up to Coach, turn and face in the same direction as Coach was standing, fold his arms and put one hand over his mouth, and nod multiple times. He looked at him a few times, nodded some more, patted the Coach on the shoulder, then ran off.

Leadership Takeaway: Communication, relationships, being able to handle yourself in the many social situations that come your way. John did all of these in just a few short minutes. He did not close the door on communication with someone who'd just received a technical foul. He gave some space and time, and, then, when the moment was right, he embraced communication. He mostly listened and then checked in with the Coach: *Are we good?* he asked. Then he carried on with his duties in a professional manner.

Be a pro. Have difficult conversations, interactions with others when you need to, and then move on. Don't close the door to communications with others. Give space and time, and then, when appropriate, revisit that conversation in a professional manner. Thanks, John, for this leadership lesson.

57. Don't f%$# it up!

Unlike many of the stories in the book, I can't remember the specific game or place or who said it, but I heard a bunch of times from top, veteran refs over the years: Don't f%$# it up! It was said in pre-game; it was said while getting dressed; it was said right before we ran onto the court, and even in the last seconds of a game. Pretty simple directions and not difficult to understand. It did take time, however, to put into practice.

After years of hearing, and now giving this directive, I break it down to the following:

- *Call what you have in front of you, the obvious.*

- *Slow it down, and breathe.*
- *Call the rules.*
- *Be aware of the game: the score, the setting, the players.*
- *Know what has happened earlier.*
- *Be bold, be strong, be fearless, be ready.*
- *Manage major moments.*

Leadership Takeaway: I think this is great advice, and I actually give it to school leaders now when I help coach and lead them. When you first hear it, it could be a little nerve-racking, yet now, after years of experience, it is pretty direct. Do your job, get what you have in front of you right, don't come up with some crazy _____ in the big moments, etc. It became a phrase of focus for me, almost like a Pavlov's dogs' situation. When I heard the phrase, it totally made me focus, settled my breathing, and dialed me in to do an outstanding job. Great advice. I recommend it to you.

58. Points of emphasis.

The NCAA started using this concept in the 2000s, when they came out with the rules each year. Yes, there was the whole rule book, and, yes, there were new rules, but the points of emphasis were the three or so points they wanted us to really focus on, hammer home. They were clearly defined, talked about in each video review and conference call, and expected to be put into practice on a consistent basis.

I liked the concept because, instead of having a giant focus on the whole rule book (you still have to know all the rules), it helped narrow down your focus and everyone's attention on these specific points. It also set a clear expectation for everyone: coaches, media, supervisors, players, and the refs that these points are to be called. Period.

Leadership Takeaway: I began to implement this practice into my leadership as a school leader. Instead of having a massive focus to kick off the school year, after collaboration and communication with stakeholders, we'd create yearly points of emphasis. We'd pick three points and have laser focus on them. I'd open every assembly and meeting with them, and had them on display throughout the year to keep coming back to them to keep them in the forefront of the work we were doing.

Like refereeing, it helped me focus on the work that I was doing to move the school forward as the Principal. All stakeholders knew what we were focusing on and what was expected. In your line of leadership, I urge you to, in collaboration with your team/staff, create these yearly points of emphasis.

59. The wise old man.

By Andrew Maira, teacher, husband, father, referee, and business owner. Andrew is my pisane from Staten Island, New York. We came up together, worked together, succeeded, and failed together. He is one of my closest friends in the officiating world, and I am grateful to him for his contribution to this book.

In 1996, I began my teaching career at Kennedy HS in Paterson, New Jersey (I started my 26th year in the same building in September 2021). In 1997, I began my officiating career refereeing HS basketball, and, in 2021–2022, I'm still officiating basketball at the Division I level.

Around the year 1999, my twin brother and I became entrepreneurs; we started a maintenance company "Twins Window Cleaning, LLC." During our start-up with Twins Window Cleaning, my brother and I would bust our humps cleaning windows—at least ten homes each weekend—trying to generate business and book up for the next weekend.

During one hot summer Saturday while at one of our customers' homes, a neighbor, an older gentleman, sat in his driveway observing my brother and me clean windows. He watched and listened to us handle all the questions from the customer/homeowner onsite. After we completed that home, and before we loaded the ladders on the truck, the older gentleman came up to us and said, "I love the way you guys really pay attention to detail. Take it from me,

if you can handle the customers that way, you'll be in business for a very long time time." Thinking we were picking up a new customer, the older man continued, "I just retired after forty years of cleaning windows and will recommend to all my customers to use Twins Window Cleaning." We were thrilled, picked his brain some more, and continued onto the next home.

Leadership Takeaway: I took that advice from the wise old man, put it in my pocket, and never forgot. *"If you can handle the customers that way, you'll be in business for a very long time."* It resonated with me and spread into every aspect of my life from being a dad, husband, referee, teacher, and business owner.

Effective communication is the healthiest ingredient in any relationship. Handling customers on a daily basis, dealing with disgruntled coaches and players on the court, teaching HS students, their parents, colleagues, communicating with my wife and daughter. My success on the court (more than 20 years), in business (22 years), and in the classroom (25 years) comes down to being an effective communicator.

For that, I owe it to *the wise old man.*
Andrew Maira

6
TRUTHS

"Rather than love, than money, than fame, give me the truth."
—Henry David Thoreau

60. Check the tape.

I learned a lot on the court as well as off the court by reviewing game film. This process helped me to look within and look at my actions in response to the actions of others. I love the concept of E + R = O: Event plus response equals outcome. The process of reviewing a game film is the process of reviewing your response to what happened out on the floor. Too many times out there, leaders blame others for what's happening or what's not happening under their watch. I say check the tape so that you can look at yourself first and then see the whole play.

Leadership Takeaway: Obviously, in real life, you do not get a recording of all your interactions each day: your body language, behaviors, your decisions. For a second, imagine you did. What would you see? In my role as a school Principal, I always encourage teachers to record themselves while teaching. It reveals so much, and the tape doesn't lie. Sometimes, we tell ourselves what we want our truths to be, instead of seeing what's really in front of us.

Because of time and training as an official, I have learned to "run the tape back" in my real life. I ask myself the question, *How could I have done it better? Where did this go sideways? What is a different word choice or timing I could have used?* Checking the tape in real life allows us to:

- *Slow it down and take a closer look.*
- *Reflect on our own actions before we look at the actions of others.*
- *Get a visual of what it really looks like.*
- *Look ahead until the next time, when maybe I can implement some changes I'd like after seeing the tape.*

I suggest, if you are able to film yourself in your next meeting, talk, or presentation, to get a deep look. If you are unable, during some self-reflection, envision what your performance looked like, and give yourself some pointers for next time. #checkthetape

61. Perception.

I learned the importance of perception very early on in my officiating career. While there are many who live their lives with that "I don't care what others think" attitude, this cannot be the case, whether it is in officiating, education, or your professional life. People are watching and making their own assumptions based on what they see. Many thoughts and perceptions can be inaccurate and off-base, but most times, people's perceptions can become reality.

There were many scenarios my supervisors would review with us and ask us, "What do you think?" The referee complaining about the coach he just officiated while he's on the plane and a booster of that same team is sitting directly behind him. The referees sitting in the hot tub the night before the game with a number of bottles of alcohol and beer around the jacuzzi with a game the next day. An official showing up to the game looking raggedy, not dressed professionally, unshaven, etc.

What do these scenarios make you think? What are your thoughts when you hear them? These scenarios can give people a bad perception of you—that you're not prepared for the game, that you're hung over, or that you're just not giving your all because of something they saw.

Leadership Takeaway: Don't give people a reason to take shots at you. Control the controllables. Be on time, keep your mouth shut when in public, and do the right thing on and off the cameras. You are a professional. You are a leader. People are watching. What is it that you want them to say about you? That you were a pro and always prepared? I like those words.

We had a speaker one time at one of our officiating clinics who hammered home the concept of the *headline test*. What if your actions were in the headline of tomorrow's newspaper? What would it say about you? These scenarios and situations really hit home with me, and I have put them into my work not only as a former official but also as a school professional. I am very mindful and aware of people's perceptions and work hard to give off the right message wherever it is that I land.

62. I'm not as bad as what they told you.

November 28, 2009, UMass vs Michigan State, Legends Classic, Atlantic City, New Jersey.

A pre-season tournament game in Atlantic City. There was a buzz in the crowd of fans from both teams who probably spent a lot of time at the beach, casino, and bar (and maybe not in that order). Fun, upbeat music blared from the speakers as the teams warmed up. One of my partners had reffed in the Big Ten for many years and knew the head Coach Tom Izzo. Tom is a well-respected Hall of Fame-winning coach. Like many, he is passionate about his team, sometimes with fiery exuberance. We chatted a little about the coaches in the pre-game because they might not know us as well as during the regular season, when coaches are used to seeing the men and women who work the conference games more regularly. Yet, there was no specific "watch out" for this or that about either coach.

The game got rolling, and I had a tough play that went against Michigan State. Coach Izzo did not like the call and protested. I ran to him and listened. I didn't even say anything as he was complaining about the call, and then he motioned for me to come closer. He softly said to me, "I'm not as bad as what they told you." I smiled at him and shared that there was only respect for him from me and the other officials. We moved on, and the game went smoothly the rest of the way.

Leadership Takeaway: Most people *do* care what you think of them and their reputation. No official had said anything bad about Coach Izzo on that day to me, yet he might have believed they did. Take people at face value, and don't believe everything you hear.

When I was hired at Port Jervis, my Principal at the time asked me the question in my interview, "If I called _____ (a past place of employment), what would they say about you?" I shared that it would probably not be good, as that supervisor and I did not see eye to eye on the discipline of the students in that school.

Well, the Principal did call, and she did indeed speak poorly of me, yet Tony DiMarco, the former Principal, saw past what she said. He believed in me, treated me for who I was and not what he heard. He finally asked her, "Do you have anything nice to say about him? Because I am going to hire him!" And I am so grateful for Tony for believing in me. Take people at face value, and don't believe everything you hear.

63. Excuses: the flat tire.

I never was late to a game. I just wasn't. I was always thinking something would happen or I might take a wrong turn, so I always built in extra time. I did, however, hear many excuses for why guys were late. It happened more than you would think. I kept my mouth shut, yet I was shocked at how some guys could be careless with their arrival times to games.

As the kids got older, and I got more familiar with the travel, I started to have less and less extra time. A diaper change here, who left their bag there. It wasn't just me anymore, as I started to take my family to more and more games.

Well, it happened. Trip to Philly. 2.5 hours down the northeast Pennsylvania turnpike. We were about 45 minutes to the school and boom...we hit a pothole. A few seconds later, duhd, duhd, duhd. A flat! We drove an AWD mini-van that had these special, fancy tires called "run-flats" that were not supposed to go flat. Well, we got a flat. I was able to pull right into a service station located in south Jersey because it was right there off the road. We were about 45 minutes from the game, with about an hour and fifteen minutes to still get there on time.

I ran in, explained what happened, and that I was reffing a game and had to get there. The service manager was less than impressed, had a number of cars in the bays, and was not really looking to switch gears (pun intended!). I told him I had a little time to spare and would wait. I texted my partners about what was happening, and they playfully ribbed me about having such a dull, non-creative excuse, and why couldn't I make up something more interesting? I insisted I was being truthful, yet the ribbing continued.

10 minutes, 20 minutes, 30 minutes passed. Nothing. I took matters into my own hands, literally. I had the family get out of the car, and jacked up the van, and wheeled the tire up to the counter. "Please!" I pleaded with the manager to patch the tire. He did eventually stop what he was doing and repaired the tire; I put it back on, and we were off.

I peeled out of the lot and sped to the game. My kids were getting upset because I was speeding. My wife was getting upset that I was upsetting the kids. I was getting upset that I was late to the game and everyone was getting upset. #Notgood.

I arrived about 15 minutes before tip-off. My hands and face were filthy from changing the tire. My partners laughed as I ran in looking like Pigpen from *Peanuts*, and made it onto the court just in time.

Leadership Takeaway: Always be honest in your interactions and behaviors. I had a track record of being on time and consistent with my travel, so in the end, my partners and supervisor know that this experience actually happened the way I told them. My hands and face were certainly evidence of the flat. Build in extra preparation time in your work and be ready for the curveball, the hurdle, or the flat tire. This practice will allow you time to work around the problem without negatively affecting your work. If your body of work and reputation can stand up on their own, when you do have a real issue, people will believe you and understand that this was a real problem.

I enjoy using this next story when speaking to students and players trying to teach the concept of honesty and integrity.

Four friends went to the beach the last weekend of college before the semester ended. Their plan was to return to school Sunday in order to take their last final Monday morning. They were having a blast on Sunday and decided to stay Sunday night. They emailed Monday informing the professor that they got a flat tire on their travels and could take the final Tuesday morning. The professor asked about their well-being and told them that would be fine. Tuesday morning at 8 a.m., he would give them an alternative final. The friends were thrilled and happy with their decision to stay at the beach for one more night.

They arrived on time Tuesday morning and thanked the professor for his understanding. He said he understood and said because of the circumstances, it should be a pretty easy final. He separated the four friends into four different rooms and gave them their exams.

The boys were horrified when they opened the final and it was only one question: Which tire? #flattire

64. For two years you are number one with me.

This is what the legendary Mickey Crowley said to me when he hired me back in 2005 into the Patriot and Ivy leagues. These were my first Division I leagues, and it was part of the contract with them: that you would keep them number one on your priority list of accepting games for two years. Awesome. No problem. I was committed.

Fast forward a year later, and John Clougherty, the supervisor of the ACC and Colonial League said he wanted to hire me and offered me a Colonial League contract. I was pumped! John Clougherty, 12-time Final Four ref wanted me! I was in. Yes, John, I'll do it...uhhhh, wait just one second.

I remembered that clause in the Patriot/Ivy contract about staying number one on the priority list. What was I to do? How could I turn this down?

I tossed and turned for twenty-four hours, asked a few trusted friends what I should do, and then the end all, be all, in decision making: I asked my parents. They gave me the best counsel, as usual.

They said, "Andrew, you gave your word to Mickey Crowley that you would be committed for two years about the priority list, so you need to honor that." What? And tell the great John Clougherty no? Oh, my...I was so stressed.

The next day I picked up the phone and called John. He very warmly greeted me and asked, "How can I help you?" I told him I was informing him of the clause in the Patriot/Ivy contract that I was to accept their games first for two years before I could accept any other games. I held my breath.

There was a pause on the other end of the line. It felt like it dragged on into about two minutes of silence. John calmly said, *"My games come behind no one."* It was like God speaking down to me. I paused with my heart pounding in my chest. This was *John Clougherty* I was telling this to! I fumbled for my words and simply said, "John, I don't know much in this business, but I do know that I have to keep my word. I told Mickey last year that I would honor this agreement." He paused again and graciously told me that he would work around my games for one year. I breathed the biggest sigh of relief that he didn't fire me on the spot.

Leadership Takeaway: I had no idea what to do in that situation. There is no training for this, just the lessons you learned while growing up: be honest, tell the truth, and be upfront with people about your business and your intentions. I didn't want to get fired and miss that great opportunity, but I had given Mickey Crowley and the Patriot & Ivy leagues my word that I would agree to that clause. I answered John honestly and with integrity, and he worked with me. Years later, after reflecting on this scenario, I believe John had *more* respect for me afterward because I stayed true to my word. I didn't lie, try to sugarcoat it, or talk my way out of a situation. I just answered with the truth. It helped me then and still does to this day.

65. Mark it!

November 2009, intrasquad scrimmage, University of North Carolina, Chapel Hill, North Carolina.

I enjoyed doing intrasquad scrimmages when I had not met anyone on the team yet, as was the case in the fall of 2009. I had not reffed UNC before—or Hall of Fame Coach Roy Williams—so I was excited to get in front of him and the Tar Heels.

Wow, he has them running! They were a fast team, and really long. They were up and down the court, fast! I had a play where I was the official under the basket, called the lead official. I was running even with the play almost to the end line when UNC 7-foot center Tyler Zeller stepped in front of the driving player, and attempted to take a charge. It was a massive collision, and Zeller is enormous. I blew the whistle hard, processed what happened, and made the split-second decision to call a block. I pounded my fists against my hips and yelled, "block, block!"

Roy leaped up, started yelling about the play. I was stunned that he was arguing in a scrimmage. I told him I felt Zeller moved and was not set when the contact occurred. He was not happy about the call and yelled out, "Mark it!" as he walked away from me.

I asked my partner at the next dead ball about my interaction with Coach Williams and what *Mark it* meant. He explained that Coach Williams was yelling up to one of the managers who was filming to mark that play because he wanted to go back and review it. He also shared that Coach Williams believes so much in defense and wants those charges. *Oh, man*, I thought, and play continued.

The rest of the scrimmage went fine, and I did not have much more interaction with Coach Williams. I kind of forgot about the block call altogether. As we showered and were getting to leave, there was a knock at the locker room door. It was one of the UNC managers. He ducked his head in and said, "Coach Williams just wanted to let us know that you had got that block call correct, and he thought we did a real nice job today."

Leadership Takeaway: *Wow, what a class act*, I thought to myself. In that short interaction with the manager coming in, I learned the following:

- *It all matters.*
- *Someone's always watching.*
- *Coach Williams is a class act.*
- *Work hard, and do the best you can. Most times, you will get it right.*
- *Be humble when you are correct; admit when you are wrong.*

I was always impressed with Coach Williams from afar, but after that interaction, I was impressed even more. The fact he sent the manager in to share that information says a lot about him and his leadership. *#itallmatters*

---

66. Andrew, I'm sorry. I know better than that.

2008, Orange County Community College, Middletown, New York.

Loved going to OCCC because it was so close to home. I so enjoyed officiating for the legendary Paul Rickard, the longtime coach there. He was the consummate gentleman: quiet, focused, conversational, and not antagonistic with the referees. He did not yell at the refs. If he did say something, you knew you had an issue because he rarely, if ever, said anything.

A few years later, his son and assistant coach, Tom Rickard, took over the helm. Tom had been with him for many years and was excited to take over as Head Coach. Tom was a bit different from his dad. He was up off the bench often, yelling at the refs, and just different—much more involved with the referees than his dad was.

I was working his game, and Tom was just fired up. On me, with what seemed like almost every whistle, every play. I tried to engage, talk him down, yet nothing was working. At his next outburst, I verbally warned Tom to stop. That didn't work, and then I gave him a technical foul.

He was shocked—hands on his hips, looking for an explanation. I stayed away and learned not to engage soon after a technical foul. Later in the game, I found my way back over to him and was expecting to get an earful about why he was getting slighted, it's our fault, etc, etc. Instead, Tom very genuinely said to me, "Andrew, I am sorry. I know better. Thank you for the warning. I should have listened." I turned to him, quite surprised because I had never had a coach say those things to me. I said "Thanks, Tom. It's all good. Now let's play ball."

The next day I also received a short email from Tom apologizing for his behavior and telling me it would not happen again.

Leadership Takeaway: As I have written several times throughout this book, you just don't know. You don't know where your words and actions will land. Fast-forward about seven years later, and Tom Rickard applied to be my Assistant Principal at Port Jervis HS (New York). Yes, that Tom Rickard. He came highly recommended with a wealth of math-teaching experience. What stood out to me was not the technical foul, but how he handled himself afterward. He was humble, reflective, and took ownership of his actions. I saw Tom at his worst and then how he responded to that.

It is the concept of E + R= O. Event plus response = outcome. We as leaders have total control of the R in this equation, just like Tom did in that scenario. The event was the poor behavior and technical, yet it was Tom's genuine and sincere response that helped him years later down the road. Control the controllables and how you respond to different situations. You never know who's watching and how the power of owning your response can help you. Side note: Tom and I became such close friends that he

and his family are featured on the cover of my second book, *The Partnership: Surviving & Thriving.*

67. New game, new day.

This is the opposite of "I got one in my pocket for you." That's an old refereeing saying meaning when a coach was not on their best behavior or a player did something that the referee did not address in the moment that they were going to get them next time. Retribution. Payback.

I don't believe in this concept at all. I think we as leaders should address things at the moment in which they are happening. If we fail to meet these behaviors head-on with truth and authenticity and not address them in the moment, that is on us. There are no paybacks. While I do believe in karma and what goes around comes around, I do not believe in payback, especially on the court or in the educational setting.

We have tools at our disposal. We have things that we can do whether as officials, professionals, or whatever your line of work is—use the tools at your disposal to address poor behaviors or negative situations.

Leadership Takeaway: Either address negative behaviors or situations in the moment or behind closed doors, but don't go around holding a grudge with an ax to grind, frustrated that you didn't handle a situation right away. The behavior you tolerate is the behavior you accept. While it may be frustrating and difficult to deal with these challenging and sometimes outrageous situations, move on. Treat each scenario as a new day, each new situation as its own entity. Don't hold grudges, and don't hold punishment in your pocket for next time.

7
MENTORSHIP

This chapter is dedicated to all those mentors, friends, and leaders who helped not only me in my journey but also countless others. A phone call, feedback, advice, listening, support, and more.

The greatest gift is to help others along the way.
—Andrew Marotta

68. It's your call, kid.

March 2010, Richmond, Virginia, The Richmond Coliseum.

It was the Colonial Athletic Association (CAA) Playoffs; I had the 12:00 p.m. game, the first of four games that day. I am fired up, happy, and proud to be there. I'm also excited to be working with the legendary Roger Ayers, Final Four and veteran college basketball official. Some say he's got the best hair in Division I!

Roger kept a calm demeanor throughout the pregame, with some light laughs and conversations about the game ahead. I was dialed in, focused, and listening. Just trying to soak it all in. As we were walking onto the court, Roger grabbed my shoulder and said to me, "You were meant to be here. Have a good game." I appreciated that small gesture on his part, and it brought my nerves down a few notches.

The game was a fantastic competition, with both teams fighting very hard. We ran our asses off and called a great game. With under a minute left, there was a tight play, where we couldn't tell which team had touched the ball last as it headed out of bounds. I was on the play, and Roger directed us to go to the monitor (as you are allowed to review plays under two minutes on video replay). Once at the monitor, it still was hard to determine who the ball went off. Roger focused on the screen, and I was kind of frozen. He looked at me and said, "It's your call, kid." I was stunned that he was allowing *me* to make the call. He asked, "What does your gut say?" I told him who I thought should get the ball, and he said, "Then let's go with it. I agree with you." We informed the coaches, teams, and the TV crew of the call, which, of course, received a split decision from the crowd. There were loud boos, and the arena atmosphere was tight. The game came down to the last shot, and we finished the game without incident.

In the locker room after the game, we received confirmation that, indeed, we were correct in our decision. Roger gave me a wink and a nod like he knew it was right the whole time. This was very

Mentorship

comforting to me, as we always want to get the right call. I exhaled deeply and was relieved to have gotten it right when it was such a tight decision.

Leadership Takeaway: I was so impressed by Roger at that moment. He trusted me and empowered me to use my gifts and talents to make the necessary call. There are so many scenarios for different types of leaders out there, and it's important they are empowered to make those decisions from those who are above them. They are hired to lead and make decisions, and while we certainly need input from stakeholders and those we work with, it's important that these leaders are empowered to make those decisions. It is important that we, as leaders, allow those around us to

feel empowered by our actions. At that moment, Roger knew I was ready and allowed me to make the call. My guess is if he thought my call was way off, he would've stopped me, but I never sensed any doubt or hesitation from Roger. He believed in me, and it felt great to take the lead in that moment. Just like his hair gel, he is sharp, smooth, and does a great job.

While this story may seem to be about making a basketball call, to me it was more than that. It was about leadership, trust, and mentoring young people along the way. Thank you to Roger Ayers for this moment and the many others in which he guided me along the way, including sharing the best hair gel!

69. Shoulder to shoulder.

November 11, 2012, Florida Atlantic vs. the University of North Carolina, Chapel Hill, North Carolina.

It was my regular-season first game officiating at the University of North Carolina, and I was just a tad bit nervous. I was always a fan of UNC, its basketball history, and the respect it had, not only in basketball circles but also as a university and the city of Chapel Hill.

Michael Jordan and Dean Smith certainly helped to raise this reputation to the highest of levels, and as a youngster, I was a huge fan. Yet on this day, as a basketball official, I was focused on doing a good job, and not being a fan of any team (except the one in black-and-white stripes). The routine for the officials (who were required to be there two hours before the game) was to stretch and relax in the locker room, review the point of emphasis for the game,

Mentorship

talk about roles and responsibilities, and then be on the floor 20 minutes prior to tip-off.

Traditionally if two or more of the referees were friendly, they would catch up about family and friends, recent games, and have a light conversation over the course of those two hours, and maybe even into the 20 minutes before the game. While I knew my two partners, I certainly wasn't friends with them, and I anticipated the two of them would be staying near each other for the 20 minutes before tip-off, while I stood at the other end in my umpire #2 position, supervising the visiting team.

As we entered the massive arena, there were 20,000 fans dressed in Tarheel classic light-blue and white. There was excitement on the floor with the players warming up, the TV crews, the cheerleaders, and staff personnel for each team running around doing their jobs. As I took my position supervising the visiting team, the head referee walked over to me and stood looking in the other direction, yet was so close that his shoulder was almost touching mine. He was inches away from me with his arms crossed, standing up tall, and watching the center court. He didn't say much; we had some light conversation, yet he stood close by me. This surprised me because I knew he was good friends with the other official, yet he chose to stand next to me. With about two minutes to go, he patted me on the rear end and said, "You good?" I replied, "Ready to go!" He said, "I know you'll do a good job tonight," and he said to lead us over to the teams. I walked forward with my shoulders back and head held high, beaming with excitement, as I approached the benches to say "Hi" to the coaches and start the game.

Leadership Takeaway: At that moment, I didn't really think about what that head referee did, but years later I reflected upon it. Watching game after game, as veteran referees would stand next to each other chit-chatting, while the newbie stood down at the other end of the court, on his own, with his mind wandering. The head referee on this occasion showed me support, bumped up my confidence level (just by his presence), and let me know he was there for me without saying anything. He is a true class act, and I told his son the story years later, about what a good man his dad is.

I learned a lot from that experience and made sure that I supported younger officials throughout my tenure. I also carry this lesson with me working with teachers and young school administrators. They may be nervous during different situations that can occur. I really didn't have to say much—just be there to support them. Just be there in close proximity, without judgment, and without directing every little thing. Just be there for support, giving the mindset of calm, and we can handle anything. There are many different ways to show support and help those who may not have been in those moments before. Maybe they don't know how to act like they have been there. At that moment on that floor at the University of North Carolina, that head referee showed me not only about support but about leadership and about kindness, too.

70. Bring in the cooler.

December 20, 2008, Virginia Tech vs. Columbia, Madison Square Garden, New York City. This is part two (tip 18) of the story of my first game at the Garden with Tim Higgins.

We had the first of two games that afternoon—Virginia Tech versus Columbia University from the Ivy League at the famed

Mentorship

Madison Square Garden. It was a high-paced game with Virginia Tech pulling away down the stretch and winning not a very close game. I loved the whole experience. The bright lights of the Garden, the TV, and certainly my partners, especially Tim. Tim was funny, gracious, and in charge of everything about that afternoon. I felt as if nothing could or would go wrong with Tim around.

Near the end of the game, Tim asked me, "What are you doing after the game?" I had mentioned that my family was there and that we were gonna watch some of the second game and go out to dinner. He said he was doing the same but maybe we could sit for a little bit after the first game. I told him that would be great.

As we ran off the floor, one of the managers of Madison Square Garden was escorting us to the locker room. Tim said to the young man, "Bring in the cooler." I thought Tim was requesting ice for his knees or feet. Shortly thereafter, the young man came back with a cooler filled with a variety of different beers. Our other partner had to be somewhere shortly after the game, and the second game of the afternoon was kicking off, so those referees left, and it was just he and I. I asked him, "Tim, you are going out to dinner with your family after the game? You've been doing this forever, and they still meet you to go out to dinner after the game. How did you accomplish this?"

I thought this was awesome and was thoroughly impressed that his family was still meeting him after games all these years. I asked, "How have you been able to make it possible that you're still doing that?" He said, "I'll tell you exactly how." Tim launched into one of the most meaningful dialogues that I had had with a fellow official about how to not only maintain my marriage and family life throughout this avocation but to make it great. To make my family part of what I was doing, he shared so much and offered the following tips:

- *Hire a babysitter every Wednesday and Saturday for my wife, who was home tending to our young kids. He said to interview the babysitters and pay them five dollars more than they were getting from any other babysitter; that way, you can get access to them all of those days.*
- *He said to make sure your wife always knows where you are, where you are going, and what time you'll be home. And when you arrive home, it's not downtime—it's time for you to come alive. It's time for you to do your share of the cleaning and do your share of being with the kids. Back to being a parent, not an exhausted referee who just got back from traveling and stressful games.*
- *He said you give your wife at least one check a year and allow her to do with it whatever she wants. You support your wife in many different ways, and, since she is allowing you to be all over the country and out all of these nights, you ask the ways that you can support her.*
- *Bring your family when you can. Soon they will be older and will not want to come, but when they are young, bring them as much as you can.*

It was amazing. I ate it all up, wrote it down and did every one of those things and then some that Tim had recommended. This was just what my wife and I needed, because this was a really hard time for her with our kids being so young and with me being gone all the time. I was just trying to get it right on the court. I was working my butt off to advance myself and get higher-level games and continue to be successful on this journey.

At that moment it wasn't about the calls on the floor but about making sure my personal life was in good order and that my family felt loved and supported. If I were to be successful on the court, I needed to make sure that they were being successful off the court as well. His advice was invaluable then and still is now, as I have begun to travel again, speaking and coaching principals and school leaders around the country.

71. Now we can play.

December 30, 2011, St. Bonaventure at Niagara, the Gallagher Center, Niagara, New York.

The battle of the Catholic schools in upstate New York. It was a freezing night in New York with two hot teams. The gym was packed and rocking. A DJ was playing during warm-ups, and the place was bumping! Bonnies (as they are called) had an NBA prospect on the team, Andrew Nicholson. This is the Duke/North Carolina game of the region and a longtime rivalry.

I was working with an old-timer from Philadelphia. He'd probably reffed this game fifty times and knew how to handle himself. I had a ton of respect for him and knew we were in good hands that night.

It was electric right before tip-off. Niagara did *not* have a huge arena at the time, the Gallagher Center. It was more like an old high school gym, with large bleachers on each side. The place was shaking, and I was ready for anything. The ball went up, and we went down to one end, and there was a quick foul from the veteran ref. We went the other way, the same thing. I thought to myself, *Wow—those came quick.* Next time down each end, same result: quick foul, which then brought us to the media timeout. The three refs came together in the middle and the head veteran ref, who'd called all the fouls, said, "Now, we can play!" and walked away.

Leadership Takeaway: On the long, cold drive back to Pennsylvania that night, I reflected on the head ref's actions. Why did he do that? Why did he insert himself into the game like that at that moment? It certainly was intentional on his part, and after thinking about it (and now writing about it, years later), he demonstrated so many leadership strategies in just those four minutes:

- *Reading the temperature of the room.*
- *Using the available tools to help: the rules.*
- *Being assertive.*
- *Being bold.*
- *Showing no fear.*
- *Taking the lead.*

I learned a lot that night. How to manage major moments. Maybe that was not everyone's style, but it was certainly his that night. His actions did indeed calm the game down. The calls did take the aggressiveness out of the players just enough that we did have a smooth game from there. It broke the tension, took away the unnecessary physicality, and refocused the players.

When the scenario in front of you calls for you to step up and take action, do just that: take action. Use the tools and experience you have to make the right call! It helped us out that cold night in Niagara, New York.

72. I saw you last night.

I was standing at the door greeting the students as they entered the HS on Monday morning. Many were dragging their feet tired with the week in front of them. Then came in Nick Chuckran. Nick looked electric...pumped up about something. He quickly approached me with a wide-eyed stare, shaking his head back and forth. As he put his bag down, he was fumbling to get something out of it, while excited to say something to me. The words struggled to exit his mouth... "You, you...you were on TV...I saw you last night...At UNC." He was speaking to me like he was in shock, shaking as the words were coming out. "How, how...are you here now? I mean, I, I knew...um, you reffed, but not like that...not like UNC...and, and on TV and all. It was awesome!"

He reached in his bag and took out a framed 5x7 picture of me reffing the game *from the night before*. He had taken a picture of his TV screen, ran to Walmart, got it developed, and brought it to me. He was so proud and happy to give it to me. I was so humbled by his words and his reaction to seeing me the very next morning.

Leadership Takeaway: As I have written many times in this book, you just never know. You never know where your influence and inspiration will land. Your actions and behaviors have a far-reaching audience, even further now with the power of social media. Someone, somewhere is always watching, and you can touch their hearts and minds with your gifts. In this heartwarming story, it was Nick.

Nick is a lifelong Carolina fan. He wore Tarheel blue almost every day and loved the 'Heels. His Dad also loved the Tarheels, and Nick and his Dad were very close. Sadly, Nick lost his Dad during his High School years, and this was very challenging for his whole family, especially Nick. He and his Dad, Tom, bonded through basketball and the Tarheels.

Through my connections of refereeing, I was able to build a relationship with Nick talking hoops, talking officiating, talking about his own playing career, and certainly his Dad, Tom.

At that moment, when he brought the photo to me, I felt so proud and humbled. He was treating me like he'd just met Michael Jordan. I was happy that my refereeing could positively influence the lives of just one of my students. I always tried to keep my "away from school refereeing business" exactly that—away from school. Nick, at that moment, brought it into school. He shared with many how "cool" it was that his Principal was a Division I college hoops ref, and he followed him on TV. I'd always liked that kid prior to this moment, but after this and when Nick's Dad passed away, I hoped that I could be a shoulder for Nick to lean on. Someone he could talk to and bounce things off. Nick felt more connected to UNC because I had been on the court, rubbing shoulders with the players and interacting with the great Roy Williams. I am grateful to Nick for his passion for hoops and the fact that it uplifted him that I reffed at that level.

Nick's Take:

By Nick Chuckran. Nick is my former student and Port Jervis HS (New York) graduate. He is a hoops fan, a loyal and hardworking young man, and obviously, a huge Carolina fan.

Mentorship

As a passionate UNC fan, you cling to anything and everything about the school. Whether it's the players past or present, the coaching staff, the Dean Dome, UNC basketball was holy territory for my father and me. Growing up with the initials "N.C.," I didn't really have much of a choice about who I would be rooting for when it came to college basketball.

The night of the North Carolina vs. Clemson game, I sat down with my father to watch the game in our usual spots. We had a routine: we would sit in the same spots in the living room while we watched the game and wouldn't move until the game was over, no matter what. When it came to UNC basketball, our superstitions outweighed reality: if we move, we lose. Fast forward to tip-off, I noticed a familiar person on the television screen. This caused me to do the unthinkable—I ran from my spot on the couch and moved as close to the television screen as possible. "Is that who I think it is?" I exclaimed to my father in excitement. There he was, reffing my North Carolina Tarheels, my Principal, Mr. Marotta. I quickly ran and grabbed my phone, scanning the television screen to hopefully capture this moment. I snapped the picture! There it was on my phone, a picture of Mr. Marotta making a call by the out-of-bounds line. I raced upstairs to my mom and begged her to drive me to Walmart so I could print out the picture. I didn't even care to watch the game anymore—I mean, how could I? I ended up printing out the picture and bought a frame for it. This was special to me, someone I looked up to was living out their dream at such a high level. When I saw Mr. Marotta the next day, I was so proud to give him the picture. He was someone who'd always believed in my abilities on the basketball court and really helped solidify that belief I had in myself. It was only right that I showed my belief in him as a high-profile Division I basketball referee.

73. Money out of your wallet.

One of the things I enjoyed the most over my time as an official was to hear the best ones talk at conferences and camps. They were not in their stripes, they were not on the court, and there was no pressure of a game looming just minutes away. It was just great referees talking about their craft and sharing successful tips. My friend Dr. Rob Gilbert, a sports psychologist from Montclair State University, always says that success leaves clues. So, when these guys were talking, I was listening because I wanted to be just like them: great officials passing on wisdom to others.

Jim Burr, a longtime Division I official and one of the best college basketball officials, talked one day in New Jersey. The question he was asked was, *How do you deal with difficult coaches?* Jim made the comparison to them taking money out of your wallet. He said if you were interacting with somebody who is trying to take money out of your pocket, would you address them? Would you tell them to stop reaching into your pocket? Would you tell them to back away? What would you do? He continued pressing on how if someone was trying to take money out of your pocket. Then he said that, when coaches misbehave, they're not necessarily trying to take money out of your pocket, but if you don't manage that coach and their behavior, you are going to lose games, which, in turn, means that you will lose money. I had never looked at it that way before or even thought about that coaches' poor behavior could be related to money coming out of my wallet.

Leadership Takeaway: You need to address the problems head-on that you are facing. Whether it is in your school, community, or workplace. If these things have a negative effect on you and your work, you must address them. The magical question is: How? How do you do it, when do you do it, and in what manner?

There's no perfect answer for this question. I urge you to watch Malcolm Gladwell's Ted Talk on spaghetti sauce. He shares in this awesome story-telling that there's no one perfect spaghetti sauce. It's a great resource. Just like this story, there is no perfect way, just the best, right way in that situation. You can check it out here:

Here are some things that you can do to address your problem just as I would've addressed the coach:

1. *Go to them directly, and tell them to stop in a respectful and professional manner.*
2. *Ask an assistant coach or someone else to speak to them. Correction maybe doesn't always have to come from you. Someone else might have a different angle or style than you that could work.*

3. Use the tools at your disposal that you have for addressing this person or the situation. In a basketball-game setting, it's a technical foul or a warning. In a professional setting, it's a letter of reprimand or a counseling memo or some other professional way of addressing poor behavior.

4. Lastly, get rid of the problem. The last resort in college basketball is ejecting the coach. That's a big play in the game, but sometimes it is necessary if the coach is unable to calm down or stop the behavior. Sometimes you have to go to these extremes in your life as well to address these problems.

74. You're on scholarship tonight, kid.

Wednesday, March 19, 2008: First-round NIT game, Cleveland State at Dayton, Dayton, Ohio.

The second story from this game, my first NIT playoff game. Working with two veterans of the game, both class acts, Tim Clougherty of North Carolina and Jim Haney from Pennsylvania. When I received the assignment, I got a call minutes later from Jim. He congratulated me on the assignment, told me where to book a room, and that he would be picking me up.

Both guys were terrific, knowing that it was my first NIT assignment: leading, advising, and guiding me all the way. At the end of the game, Jim said, "Let's grab a bite afterward." Absolutely.

Jim drove and picked the place and the table. When we sat, he generously said, "Don't even think about paying. You're on scholarship tonight, kid!"

Leadership Takeaway: I was on scholarship in a lot of ways that night: advice, support, direction, and financial. The guys couldn't have been nicer, including buying me a beer and food afterward. Jim knew it was a first for me, and he went out of his way to make it special. We nailed the game and acted like pros before, during, and afterward.

When working with newer folks, put them on scholarship. Show them the way, go out of your way to support them, treat them, and more. It was nice for me to receive this on that evening, but even nicer when I was able to pay it forward to others, saying those special words: "You're on scholarship tonight, kid!"

75. What can I do to get better?

I always enjoyed working with younger, less-experienced officials, especially when they wanted to get better. When I became a member of the ACC and Atlantic-10 rosters, people really started to reach out to me, asking how I did it, and what were some techniques that I practiced to be successful. They, too, wanted to reach that level, and I love the growth mindset.

I was working at a local spring HS league, and a local official asked the magic question: "Andrew, how can I get better?" I liked this official, his attitude, and his work ethic. I told him we'd work some games, and then I'd sit down with him to discuss.

We grabbed a beer after the game, and I asked him, "What do you think you need to work on to get to the next level?" He shared a number of technical topics related to placement, call selection, etc. I listened intently and asked him, "Anything else?" He could not offer any other suggestions.

I told him that all of his suggestions were good, but they were minor. There were a few global, bigger items he needed to adjust first, and I asked him if he was ready to receive some real feedback. I further explained that I was saying this respectfully, authentically, privately and that some of it might be difficult to hear—and was he still ready? He paused, smiled hesitantly, and said, "Yes, I am ready."

I laid it out for him that he had the right attitude and mindset to *want* to do a good job. That was a big first step. I told him he needed to lose weight, show tremendous confidence without being obnoxious, and his signals and speed on the court needed to be academy award-winning in style and performance. He digested this and talked more about his game.

Fast-forward eight months to the next season, and this official was totally renewed. He had lost sixty pounds, was chiseled, more confident, and ready to go. He thanked me profusely for our conversation and the feedback. He shared, "I could not have done this without you!" I replied, "I didn't lift one weight with you or pull one donut out of your mouth. You did it on your own. I just shared with you what people maybe were afraid to say to you because they were afraid they might hurt your feelings."

Leadership takeaways: Your feedback is tremendously important to others. I knew that this person was *ready* to receive the feedback because they wanted to really get better. I did the best I could to be respectful, honest, and authentic with him in our conversation. All of the stuff he was talking about—placement, positioning, call selection, etc.—were all minor tweaks to his work, yet his weight, his confidence, and speed, and mechanics needed an overhaul. People needed to *believe* his calls, and, simply put, you are more believable when you look the part. So much of leadership is looking and acting the part, and that's what he needed.

I was so proud of him (and still am) that he took action on my advice, implemented change in his professional and personal life, and got himself into great shape. Not only did he advance on the basketball court, but he also advanced in several other areas…the confidence carried over outside of basketball. This is another prime example of the crossovers of leadership from our advocations to all parts of our lives. Have the courage to give people the *real* feedback they need, and do it in a respectful, authentic, confidence-building way. Build people up—don't break them down.

---

76. Give him a chance, Coach.

I had many a mentor use those words toward a coach when they were reffing with me when I was starting out. People did not know me, did not trust me. Those simple few words from a veteran official went a very long way in helping me build trust. If a veteran official was willing to let the coach know I could do it and make that statement, *"Give him a chance,"* most did. That official was putting his rep on the line to assist me, so I knew I'd better step up and do the job.

They could say things like, "Yeah, Coach, I don't really know this guy…let's see" or even, "No, Coach, never worked with him before." *Give him a chance* is saying a few things:

- *He/she is new; give them some space.*
- *I know they can do the job; give them a little time.*
- *I'm comfortable with this new ref out here; you should be, too.*

Leadership Takeaway: Being a mentor and showing leadership isn't always some grandiose occasion, yet many times it is in these simple interactions, simple communications that leadership is displayed. This little phrase, "Give him a chance, Coach" can do so much. Think about when you are leading a team, and the new guy/girl shows up. People are wondering, "Is this person any good? Can they do the job?" and so on. Set the tone early and give them a chance.

I felt proud to use those words when I started working with some younger guys and could say that phrase to a coach. It showed my trust in the newer official and politely asked him to back up, back off, and give some space. Do this for some younger folks in your organization when they are getting started.

---

77. There is a reason why they are called legends.

By Dan Spainhour. Dan is a coach, mentor, writer, and friend. He spent thirteen years coaching at Bishop McGuinness and West Stokes HS in North Carolina. He also assisted at the University of Miami with Coach Leonard Hamilton for three years both at Florida State and the University of Miami. He is the creator of The Leadership Publishing Team, which produces the monthly The Coaching and Leadership Journal. *to which I am a happy subscriber. I have used the stories in his book,* Leading Narratives, *so many times in my talks over the years. Learn more at leadershippublishingteam.com.*

In my third year as a head basketball coach, our team was invited to the prestigious Alhambra Catholic Invitational Tournament in Maryland. Each year the tournament invites eight of the top Catholic High school teams in the nation to participate. To say the least, we were ecstatic to receive an invitation. Our school community was proud that our program had reached such a level as that.

Mentorship

I was excited about being around some of the top coaches in the country—especially Ray Mullis of Baltimore Cardinal Gibbons and the Hall of Famer Morgan Wootten of Dematha. I must admit I felt a little out of place, since I was so young, and there were so many legends in the tournament. The opening day of the tournament called for a breakfast in the banquet room of the hotel where everyone was staying. I was told we would have breakfast, and then the coaches would be interviewed afterward. I expected a relaxed event so I went downstairs in my team warmups. As I got off the elevator, I saw Morgan Wootten surrounded by a group of people. He was in a suit and tie. I didn't think anything of it—thinking he probably had some TV event to do; after all, he was in the Basketball Hall of Fame.

Coach Wootten saw me and stepped away from the group and motioned for me to come over. He graciously reached out his hand, and we shook hands. He took me aside so we could talk one on one and said, "Coach Spainhour, you may not know, but this event is always pretty formal. It is as if the whole town comes out, and there will be plenty of TV cameras. I just want you to know."

"I had no idea," I said. "I thought we were just having breakfast and doing a few interviews with some newspaper guys."

"No, it's a pretty big deal. I just wanted you to know."

"I should probably change, shouldn't I? Do I have time?"

"That's up to you. I know that, as the new team here, you will be the first coach to speak, but I'll offer to go first if you aren't back in time."

I hurried back upstairs and put on my suit that I was going to wear for that evening's game. I raced back downstairs and made it just as the program was beginning. Coach Wootten had saved me a seat next to him on the dais, and I sat down, now appropriately dressed, next to the coaching icon.

I have thought of this event a few times throughout my career. Coach Wootten could have very easily let me go into the banquet hall dressed as I was. Instead, he did what great leaders do—he saw something/someone who needed assistance, and he went out of his way to give it. He even made it easier by offering to go in my place if I wasn't back in time. He did not force me to do anything and left the decision completely up to me. But he offered his wisdom, and it was up to me to choose to accept it or not. I'm so glad I did.

The same traits that made Morgan Wootten a great coach also made him a great leader and person. I am thankful that our paths crossed.

78. Wow, you held the ball.

I'm a big fan of "the power of a single experience" mindset. The idea that one interaction, one experience can deeply impact the life of the other person with whom you are interacting. One of my favorite things to do as an official was during downtime: a dead ball, a timeout, etc., I would always ask a child to hold the ball. Such a simple thing, right? But in looking at it through the eyes of the child and the parent, you literally connected them to the game. The kid actually got to touch the ball. Feel the sweat, the smell of the leather, and feel like he touched a college basketball game. I always enjoy those moments. I usually made sure I spoke with the parents a little bit and shared the fact that I have little children, too, and that I miss them while on the road. I would

Mentorship

offer a high-five to the kid, a smile, etc. I did these small actions for a couple of reasons:

- *Brighten the life of a young child.*
- *Connect them to the game.*
- *Show all the stakeholders that the referee was human and not just a machine blowing the whistle.*
- *Always make time to smile and enjoy the company around you, especially kids.*

Leadership Takeaway: Simple acts can go a long way in brightening the lives of others. That child holding that ball at a college basketball game might remember that experience for a lifetime. You in your role as a college basketball official and/or a leader have many avenues and opportunities to positively impact the lives of those we serve. This is a small act that I believe can go a long way. Look for these opportunities in your life whether it is on the court or in your professional world—simple acts that can uplift others, especially when it is a child. #ThePowerOfASingleExperience.

8

MENTAL STRENGTH

It all begins and ends in your mind.

79. The brighter the lights.

I asked the big-timers so many times, "How do you do it? How do you make it look so easy?" I received many of the answers you would expect: It takes time, years of experience, many failures, etc. This one stood out to me: The brighter the lights, the bigger the stage, the more I slow it down. This mentor went on to explain that if you are working on the biggest stage, everything was bigger: the lights, the TV, the money, the venue, the impact, and more. His mindset was to slow it down and keep it simple. He offered many of the following suggestions:

- **Slow everything down:** *your mind, your breathing, your focus. Not your intensity and certainly not your running, but your decision-making, your thoughts, and inner workings. Slow.*
- **Keep it simple:** *same hotel, same type of car, same light meal before. Nothing to make this game seem more important than the others. Do your routine, stand tall, be confident—all the things you have done to get you to this point.*
- **Try—don't try harder:** *If you put too much pressure on yourself or try to be perfect, you will push too hard. I smile as I write this because I was guilty of this too many times: trying too hard. Do your best, and forget the rest. As I wrote many times in the book, if you miss one, get the next one... don't keep going back to the one you missed, but move forward to the next one.*

Leadership Takeaway: While it was cool and satisfying to get to those "bright lights," the best thing I could do to be successful in those moments was to keep it simple. It sounds easy and wasn't always perfect (as I have shared many times in the book), but you do the best you can. Breathe, act like you've been there before, and perform the way you have many times prior to that experience. You've got this!

80. You don't have to ref the whole game.

Many have asked over the years, *How do you do it? How do you manage it all? Being a Principal, father, ref, writer, etc.?* There was no one perfect answer, and sometimes I don't know how I did it (thanks again to my wife!!!), yet this concept was very helpful.

When I made it to the Division I level, many of the veterans told me that I did not have to ref the whole game, just four minutes at a time. Initially, I was a little confused, because I had in my mind and heart that I wanted to do a great job for the whole game: from when I got out of the car until I returned.

Leadership Takeaway: The timeouts are built into the game. So there is a prescribed timeout at the first whistle after the sixteen-minute mark, twelve, eight, and so on in addition to the ones that the coaches can call. You know those scheduled timeouts are coming, so just be perfect until that time. You can do anything for four minutes. This was very relieving for me—putting things into small, tight time containers. Do great for four minutes: awesome. Take a breath and move on to the next. Screwed it up. OK. Deep breath, tuck that mistake away and deal with it later, and move on to the next segment, the next play, the next timeout, trying not to make that mistake again.

I really like this concept and still use it today in my professional life. Smaller, more manageable chunks of time makes it easier to process, prepare, restore, and keep moving on. Check out this clip from when I was guest on *The Crown Refs Podcast* with my friend Paul Diasparra:

81. Just another game.

Be humble. A common practice among refs was to ask, "Hey, where are you going next?" or "Where were you last night?" When I started to work games in the bigger conferences, and I was with guys who weren't working those leagues, I felt bad if I shared, "I was at University of North Carolina" or "I was at Florida State," and they were at Backawards State Community College the evening before. I never wanted to act bigger or better than anyone else or as if I were "showing off." Many taught me, including my parents, to be humble and practice humility in all I do. While sometimes the guys wanted to hear about these experiences and were generally happy for me that I was working those games, I didn't feel it was appropriate at that moment, at that time, to discuss which game I had.

My Dad taught me: "SPS: Self-Praise Stinks." If anybody wanted to know where any ref was, they could just look it up on the internet. The games are very transparent in that way, and if guys really wanted to hear about some of these experiences, they could just ask. So, I tried to downplay where I was, what game I was doing, the big call, etc. Keep it simple. I did *not* want to lie to people, but I would make comments like, "Just a small local game, nothing flashy." I wanted to remain humble and stay focused on where I was right there, not where I'd been or where I was going.

Leadership Takeaway: There is no perfect way and no exact science. These were traits I picked up from people along the way when I was coming up: Be kind to others, be a mentor, be humble and more. I was very grateful and happy to officiate at that level, but I did not want to show off.

The best mindset is how you can help others along their journey. Ask questions like, "How was your game last night? Tell me more, and what were some takeaways for you?" Ask people about their work, their challenges, their journey, and while there is a time and place for them to hear from you, focus on others to help them in their journey.

82. The last season.

This was tough. The 2018–2019 season was my last season that I worked officiating college ball. I was torn between whether I should continue this journey of officiating or answer the calling of what I was feeling: helping and inspiring other school leaders through speaking, writing, and workshops. Gone were the bright lights of the ACC, Atlantic 10, and some of the other bigger conferences. I was not working in those leagues any longer. I had a few smaller Division I conferences I was still working that year, but most games were D II, D III, and junior-college games.

Think about it: going from making a big check—with a comma in it—reffing at premier colleges with games that were on national television with top referees, coaches, and teams, to places where you had to bring your own towel, your own water bottle, and shower in the supply closet with cold water and making just a couple hundred bucks. It was a tough adjustment.

I went through a period when I was down, not happy about where the refereeing was going, and not sure what to do. My book sales were climbing, speaking engagements were ramping up, and my positive influence on other school leaders was growing stronger. I was torn and felt like I was breaking up with a girlfriend who I loved and was starting to date someone new, who I also really liked.

I decided that I would hang it up. It was on Route 80, heading back east to Northeast Pennsylvania on a freezing January Saturday after being at a PSAC (Pennsylvania State Athletic Conference) game. It was a 2 p.m. game. I left at 7 a.m. that morning, drove four hours, did the game, which was a rough one (multiple technical fouls, fans going crazy, and almost a fight!), then four hours home, for only a couple hundred bucks. I arrived home at 8:30 p.m., after 13.5 hours and the cost of gas, food, drinks and one giant headache, and missing my family on a Saturday. I decided that was it. I was going to move on to writing, presenting, and having a deep impact on the lives of educators and leaders from around the country.

I also decided in that moment that I would go all out on the court for those last 25–30 games I had left. I would be totally into it and would ref each one like it was my last. When I was at Southwest Penn Community College (making this name up!), I made up in my head that I was working the Duke/UNC game on ESPN. I was totally energized, running hard, and tried to have the best attitude. I brought my kids with me when I could, tried to eat at local joints along the way, and make the memories last. I wanted to leave officiating with a positive memory and be happy and proud with what I had done.

Leadership Takeaway: It worked! I really enjoyed the last three months of that year. I engaged with my partners, was totally into the games, ran hard (even when it was not the best game) and tried to take it all in. Make the best of the situations you are in. Could I have continued along where I was? Sure, yet I decided it was time to do something different, and I ran with it. I miss the guys, the competition, and edge of the games, yet I am completely satisfied with making this life change and grateful for all that has come from it. For those last few months, I had to fake it to feel it. I manufactured that energy and enthusiasm, because my heart and mind were elsewhere. I needed to create and work hard to have focus and a clear mind. When I ran off the court that last Saturday in March 2019 at Dartmouth University, I was proud of myself and the great run I'd had.

83. Be at your best on a Tuesday night.

The Hall of Fame Coach Bob Knight used to say, "Everyone wants to win on Saturday, but not everyone wants to practice hard on Tuesday." The same applies here: everyone wants the big game on TV on Saturday, but what about Tuesday night, the smaller game, lower level, etc.? How do you bring the focus and same intensity to that game? Those kids, those fans, those coaches want the same effort and level of performance of you regardless of the circumstances or date of the event.

Leadership Takeaway: This is about you and your mental preparation toward your work, and not the work itself. Your job is to be consistent and be ready, regardless of what the event is. Your mindset is to bring it to each event, not just the big ones.

Let's make the comparison to a religious service. Does the clergy do an amazing job on a big holiday where the church is packed but just an OK job the rest of the time? Obviously no—they want to grow their membership and have people come each and every week *and* also enjoy an amazing holiday service.

A story: The head cardiologist was interviewed after surgery on President Bill Clinton and was asked, "How did it feel knowing you were operating on the President?" The doctor responded that he knew who the patient was and was proud to be doing the surgery, yet he continued that it wasn't any different than any other patient. They didn't do anything different for President Bill Clinton than they would do for any other patient.

Be consistent in your approach to your work. You should be aware of the circumstances around the events of your work, but your approach and preparation should be the same.

84. Mental strength and performance.

We eat right, we train, we get a rest. We work out, we run, we get the best equipment, we double-check times, we work on our travel, all of the things we do to prepare to be a high-level college official, to be an elite leader. We are doing so to be great at our jobs, but what do we do for our minds? How do we work out our minds and get mentally prepared for high-intensity work? Are there things we could be doing? What are some things other great leaders do to mentally prepare and train their minds? Here are a few things that work for me:

- *Mental Performance Daily podcast by Brian Cain, briancain.com*
- *The Success Hotline, by Dr. Rob Gilbert, 973-743-460 or on Ironclad*
- *ZONEfulness by Joe Dowling, University of Pennsylvania, mindfulness.com*
- *The 5SWs mindset:* the concept of **S**ometimes it **W**ill, **S**ometimes it **W**on't, **S**o **W**hat, **S**omeone's **W**aiting, **S**tick **W**ith it.

- *The #keeprolling attitude:* first cousin to the 5SWs, the commitment to just keep going, no matter what. Don't quit, can't fail. Whatever happens, just keep rolling, keep showing up, keep leading, keep learning.

Leadership Takeaway: As I wrote earlier in tip number seventy-eight about the spaghetti sauce and choice in Malcolm Gladwell's great TEDTalk: the concept of there's no one perfect formula for success or how to achieve exactly what people want in life. There's no one thing that works for leaders, but taking the things that work for you and continually doing them is one of the secrets of success. Listed in this section are just a few of the things that work for me and my mindset to keep going: to keep practicing the successful behaviors and actions that propelled me forward in my life as a former Division I men's basketball official as well as a leader, speaker, father, husband, Principal, and more. I recommend taking a look at these to see if they could work for you. The first three are resources and personal friends of mine. Each has been a guest on my #ELB Education Leadership & Beyond podcast, and I use their work daily to help me #survivethrive. Dr. Gilbert literally changed the course of my life with his success hotline that I still call and take notes on daily.

The final two listed above are just my mindsets: They keep me moving forward, they get me through hard times, they are timeless and can work for all. You just have to have a loud, strong voice in your head and heart that keeps telling you these thoughts to live by and strengthen your mind.

85. The quiet.

Being a busy professional can be quite taxing. Whether as an official, or professional, if you're leading a busy lifestyle, I urge you to take *quiet time* for yourself. It can look very different for each person, but it is taking time for yourself that is the important point. That can be at a coffee shop before your game just people-watching, it could be a meditation in the car before your big talk, it can be yoga in the morning when you wake up to set your day straight, or even just having some quiet reflection at the end of the day. Wherever it is in your day, take the time that you deserve as a busy professional to have some quiet time—some clear-thinking time for your brain as well as some breathing time for your lungs.

Try this exercise: it's called "7, 7, and 7." I learned it from my friend and sports psychologist Dr. Rob Gilbert. Get to a quiet place; you don't have to close your eyes, but it's OK if you do. Take a deep breath for seven seconds, hold your breath for seven seconds, and breathe out for seven seconds. Do that very slowly and succinctly, and feel the results. These simple twenty-one seconds can help you immensely in slowing your breathing, focusing, and just relaxing.

Leadership Takeaway: Life is short. Take time for yourself to have some quiet time. After moving out of New York City into Northeast Pennsylvania, I have fallen in love with quiet walks early in the morning all to myself. My dog, a great cup of coffee, and just my thoughts. Deep breathing, reflection, and just quiet. Start making these actions habits, and you will reap the benefits. Find the time and space for #thequiet.

86. Bench time.

I loved playing college basketball at Guilford College in Greensboro, North Carolina. I was far from a star, just a hard-working high school athlete who really wanted a chance to play college basketball. I am proud of myself for being one of the hardest workers on the team with the hope that I would get a chance to play. Every once in a while, either in a big win or ugly loss, I would get those chances. I did learn to enjoy my time on the bench as well. My teammates and I developed a rapport, I engaged in rooting for my teammates, and I really became a student of the game.

What I did not realize while I sat on that bench all that time was that I was also becoming a student of officiating. When the one ref is in a certain position, he's right in front of the bench. I watched his movements, watched his interactions with our head coach, and I also watched his response to what was happening on the court. Making the calls, interacting with the players, etc. Every once in a while, the official would even interact with us.

Leadership Takeaway: In those moments of sitting on the bench, I did not think that one day I would become a college official. I was learning and absorbing the game through their eyes. Sometimes we think the situations we are going through are just a waste. Many people become frustrated with sitting on the bench. It becomes a negative situation, players get internally frustrated, and many quit because they are not getting the playing time they think they deserve. Those thoughts never entered my mind, and, while I wish I'd played more, in the end, the whole experience wound up helping me down the road. You just never know where these situations can take you or how they can help you. Sitting on the

Mental Strength

bench all that time in Guilford did help me because I watched so many officials up-close work the game. Learn what you can from the different situations that come your way. You never know when they will help you down the road.

87. What's your best game?

My best game is the game right now. My biggest game is the one right now. My most important game is the one right now. Many people would ask me these questions and still do. These were and are my answers. The one right now, the games, players, and action right in front of me. This helped simplify things and have great focus. I wasn't thinking ahead to the next game, the next trip; my eyes and attention on what was right in front of me. Let me get this play right, in this game, right now.

Leadership Takeaway: The great Brian Cain, in his Mental Performance Daily Podcast, talks about *not* keeping his eyes on the prize, but keeping his eyes on what is right in front of him.. If you keep getting what is right in front of you *right*, you will get to the prize. You will reach your goals and get to where you want to be.

So much in today's world is in the palm of our hands—literally—in the cell phones. I have tried to keep it simple and be where my feet are. Focus on who and what are in front of me and give them my best attention. On the court, there were many distractions that could take your attention away from what you were doing. The same in life. Lock in your focus to accomplish the things you want.

Who's your best client? Your most important student? Top issue? The one right in front of you.

88. Blue and white.

This was my mindset. Blue and white, green vs. gold, red vs. black. I could not look at the games like I was reffing Syracuse vs. Cornell or Duke vs. Army. When I first started to do these bigger games in the bigger conferences, I tried to keep it simple and just keep it about two teams distinguished by colors. Not the rivalry, or the big TV game, etc.—just two teams playing ball.

When I did the Army/Navy game, the Richmond/VCU game or the backyard brawl of Scranton, the Kings/Wilkes game, or my first big TV game, the Staten Island HS classic St. Peter's vs. Curtis, I tried to bring it back down. Simplify every aspect of it all. I certainly knew the rivalry status, the bragging rights at stake, and what all these games represented for their communities. One strategy was to just go with the colors. Only look and process the colors on the jerseys, not the names that went with them.

Leadership Takeaway: There are blue and white colors in the local CYO gym as well as in the Army/Navy game for example... whatever that big event is, take away some of the "bigness" of it, and bring it back down a notch. By me referencing the colors in my mind, it took away the hype and just made it about the two teams on the floor. As I have said many times in this chapter on mental strength, it narrowed things for me and helped keep it simple: just two teams playing a game, regardless of the names on the jerseys. Get plays right, one at a time.

If you allow the "bigness" of an event to get to you and your mindset, it can bring your performance down. Make it easier on yourself, keep it simple, and adjust focus on the two colors: blue and white. Outside the basketball world, focus on the task at hand and remove the enormity of the project or job. Strip away the glamour of "it is this client or this person," and get the job done without the hype. It will bring down your anxiety as well as that of those around you.

89. Why did you give him an A rating?

I heard this story from a supervisor once at a camp, and it stuck with me. It reminds me to be courageous, be bold, and do your job, regardless of the circumstances.

The home coach was getting beat and getting frustrated. He began to take his frustrations out on the refs. He went after the one particularly hard, the ref warned him, he continued, and he wound up getting tossed (ejected from the game).

The supervisor happened to be watching the game, and he had that, "Oh, here we go..." kind of feeling. The next day he checked the report from the coaches, and this coach gave the ref who'd ejected him an A rating. The supervisor double-checked and sure enough, A rating. He picked up the phone, called the coach, and asked him about what happened. He continued asking, "OK, Coach. Thanks for explaining all that, but you gave him an A rating? How come?"

The coach explained that the ref was nothing but professional, warned him, and that he deserved to be tossed. He continued sharing that if this particular ref had the _____ to throw him out at home, then he knew the ref was too tough enough to ref him anywhere. He also said, "I know he will enforce the rules for me also when I am on the road, so he earned my respect."

Leadership Takeaway: Respect is earned in many ways. In this instance, the coach had more respect for the official *after* he ejected him because he was tough enough to enforce the rules against the home coach when he knew he was wrong. It made the coach realize that the official would do the same when that coach was on the road also, and that is what the coach wanted: fairness. Fairness, courage, and knowing how to handle yourself in a tough situation.

Doing the right thing is not a *sometimes* thing. The best leaders do it all the time, even when they might get their hands dirty. People respect strength, and this official showed strength by tossing the home coach when he was wrong. He wasn't afraid to do what he had to do at that moment. Leadership can be tough, and doing the right thing can be even tougher sometimes. In the end, most respect you for demonstrating that toughness, that leadership, especially through adversity.

90. Get right back in there and ref your a$% off.

December, 2003, Staten Island, New York.

I had just done a holiday tournament in Staten Island with a visiting team from Brooklyn. The visiting coach thought they were getting cheated and earned a technical foul. That was it. He began screaming incessantly at me and pulled his team off the court. Forfeit. Bad scene. Ugly.

When I checked my schedule when I got home, I saw it. Yup, you guessed it. Same team at their gym in Brooklyn. *Ahh, man*, I thought to myself. Probably will get switched. I called the supervisor right away. Yes, the legendary Nick Gaetani, whom you have read about multiple times in this book.

I told him what happened in Staten Island and that I had the visiting team in their gym in the next night. There was a pause on the line. Hello? I asked. Nick was a tough guy. #Oldschool. I can

Mental Strength

still hear what Nick told me ringing in my ears, and I get goosebumps thinking about it.

Nick firmly stated—in a voice that sounded like he was clenching his teeth as he said it, "You go into the gym, walk right up to the coach when it is time to shake hands, look him right in the eye, and say, 'Have a great game.' You ref your a$% off. If he says one thing, you whack him (give him a technical foul) immediately."

Leadership Takeaway: I was invigorated by his response to this situation. Inspired, motivated, and confident. I thought he would adjust, switch me, and move on. Nope. Not Nick. Not this situation. Nick forced me to meet this awkward social moment head on with courage and boldness. I didn't do anything wrong, so why should I feel out of sorts? I stuck my chin out, chest up, shoulders back, and did just that: reffed my a$% off and didn't have one problem.

Leadership, many times, puts you in weird, awkward situations that you did not cause, but because of the leader, you need to brace and deal with. Many people avoid these conflicts, but that coach needed to own his behavior from the game before. Was it the time in between? Did Nick call him and tell him to behave? Was it just a new day? I'll never know, but I was emboldened by Nick's reassurance and advice to me to do a great job. I was a good ref, and I hadn't done anything wrong. Remind yourself of that when you have to face these situations. Keep your chin up, eyes up, and be bold; you will get through them. Leadership lessons are all around us. No one said they would always be comfortable.

91. Be where your feet are.

A short meditation I used to do to get focused was to look down at my feet, and quietly say to myself, "Be where your feet are, be where your feet are." If the court was named for someone, I'd try to stand on that space, and repeat the mediation. That is where I was and where I needed to be for the next two hours. I am a busy guy: family, job, and a lot of responsibilities, but for the next two hours, I only had one responsibility. One focus. One job. One. Do an outstanding job for the game in front of me: the players, coaches, fans, universities, TV, and all the stakeholders of the game.

When I reffed, I was a HS Principal and a parent of three young children, ranging in ages from eight to a newborn. There was always something to think about: an issue at school, a sick child, a snowstorm back home, and more. For those two hours, I needed absolute focus. Shutting it all down and being in that space.

Leadership Takeaway: The feet are the reminder. They are always with you and just a glance away. Whether in a board meeting, college game, classroom, be where your feet are. I love the comparison to a submarine and the airtight compartments on a ship. You know, the ones with those big round wheels on them. Close that door tight, and turn the wheel. No leaking water, air pockets, interruptions. Just you in your space, and get the work done. Zero distractions. Even the job of writing this book. I fought the distraction demons off countless times during this journey in order to focus on what I needed to do.

Another tip is the timer: I am going to do this for _____ minutes, be it a plank for two minutes, writing for two hours, driving for four hours, or being engaged in an intense college basketball game for two hours. The timer gives you an end time to be engaged and be where your feet are for a fixed amount of time. It gives you an end goal, one you can achieve. #bewhereyourfeetare

92. Only blow if you know.

Learned this concept from the great Art Hyland, longtime supervisor of the Big East conference. I never cracked the lineup for the Big East, and that was something that I'd always wanted. I grew up watching St. John's with my parents, as they were both alumni. Those classic battles of Syracuse and Georgetown and Villanova and UConn and Pitt. It seemed like those games were always on TV; it was the heart of college basketball as I grew up.

I finally got to the tryout camp, and I learned quickly that this was one of Art's mindsets. This, in turn, became a mindset of his officials: *Only blow if you know.* Simply put, if you were 100% sure of what you had, blow the whistle. If you weren't sure, leave it alone. This was an example of an error of omission being better than an error of commission. If you did not blow the whistle, the game would continue, and maybe the player would score or continue as they were without you blowing the whistle. When you blow the whistle, everything stops, and everyone looks at you, so it's important that you are right. This took a lot of time and discipline over the years to learn this after having blown the whistle and having been wrong too many times. When a crowd of 10,000+ rains down on you, you learn quickly that it's important to get them right.

Leadership Takeaway: Simply put: when you blow the whistle, be right. In your life, when you have to make decisions, call the obvious ones and get the obvious situations right. If it is unclear or you are unsure, maybe hit pause for a night or two. Maybe sleep on it. Maybe ask someone else what they think a solution could be. These are all alternatives to rushing into a decision that you are unsure of.

Making hard decisions is part of the role as a leader. When the decisions with the calls are clear, they are easy. It's the ones that are unclear where, maybe, we *do* have to hit pause. It is an art, not a science, and it is a learned skill. Be patient with yourself, and continue to learn from the mistakes that you make as a leader. *Only blow when you know.* This mindset and leadership strategy will keep you making good decisions for a long time.

9
BE READY

*I'll be ready. I am not sure for what exactly.
But maybe that is what ready really means.*
—Holly Goldberg Sloan

93. The play is coming to me.

I remember as a kid playing little league, and the coach would tell us all to think that the ball could be hit to each one of us on any play. Be ready for the ball to be hit to *me*. This mentality kept me engaged in the game, and I did tell myself to be ready that the ball was coming to me each time it was pitched.

I carried the same mindset with me as I began officiating. It kept me ready and focused on the game, especially at the end of the game. Most coaches would call a timeout near the end of a close game to set up a play. The refs would also get together to discuss a likely scenario, prep for anything, and be ready. I always walked out of those huddles with the mindset of *the play is coming to me*. I would do the following when I had a few moments to collect myself:

- *Take a deep, long breath.*
- *Envision me making the right call.*
- *Slow it all down and process before I made any motions.*
- *Take it one play at a time.*

Leadership Takeaway: When you are ready to receive the work, the play, or whatever it is coming your way, you can be prepared to receive it and do a good job. If your mindset is *I hope this doesn't come my way*, then you are preparing for failure. *Be ready and wait vs. wait to get ready.*

If you consistently tell yourself that the next big thing is coming to you, you will always be ready and develop an *I've got this* attitude. This leads to confidence, preparedness, and the readiness you want on the court, in business, and in leadership.

94. The knock at the door.

November 24, 2012, JMU vs. Miami of Ohio, Oxford, Ohio.

It was a cold, rainy Saturday in Ohio. It wasn't snowing, but it was bone-chilling cold, and it was the Saturday after Thanksgiving.

Be Ready

The students were not on campus—no band, no cheerleaders, no TV. It was a non-league game, and we weren't anticipating a lot of hype or fanfare. Really, it was just all of us trying to get through the game—the refs and the two teams—to work off our Thanksgiving turkey. We held a pre-game conference to discuss the game, talked about our families a little, and then each took some quiet time to mentally prepare for the game.

Then came the knock at the door.

We thought it was odd because the table crew, game manager, and trainer all already had come in, so who could it have been? My partner opened the door, and John Adams, the NCAA Coordinator of Officials, walked in. *WHAAAAAT! What was he doing here?* He very warmly and professionally introduced himself, talked about the game, what he was seeing around the country, and then was off to the court area. Wow!

Leadership Takeaway: You never know when your opportunity will come. If he hadn't come in the locker room but was at the game, would I have tried as hard? Been as sharp? Focused? I certainly had those attributes and more *after* knowing he was present in the arena, but I had already trained myself to act *as if*. Act as if someone was watching. Ref like someone was there to scout me and wanted me on their roster. Be a pro, no matter the circumstances. I knew there was always a camera, always someone watching. Having the National Coordinator of Officials at my game was cool, but I was ready, whether he was there or not.

Lead regardless of your circumstances. Be at your best whether your supervisor is there or not. *Someone's* always watching, and your opportunity is waiting for you. Go get it!

John's (Adams) take:

One of the great pleasures for me during my seven-year tenure was surprising the officiating crews at games around the country. Quite often these would be at "off the radar" games like JMU at Miami Ohio on a cold, rainy Saturday afternoon. The reason I would not let the crew know I was coming ahead of time was because I was trying to create as much pressure on the crew as possible so that I could observe and evaluate their talent as part of my job to select 100 officials to start in each year's NCAA tournament. While you can't really replicate the pressure of an NCAA tourney game, you certainly can assess officiating talent in person, especially when the "boss" is in the arena and watching the game.

—*John Adams*

95. Hey, kid, will you park my car?

2002, Christ the King HS, Queens, New York.

I was working the JV game that Saturday afternoon after the big Christ the King vs. St. Raymond's varsity matchup. (Both New York Catholic HS powerhouse schools). I most definitely wanted to get there early to watch the varsity game first so I could check out the refs and learn from them. It was a big game, and the place was packed. Just finding a parking spot was a challenge. I circled around and around, and eventually found a spot. I was walking to the gym and a car sped up on me, startling me. It was the great Phil Sallustio, longtime New York City veteran ref and an all-around great guy.

He yelled, "Hey, kid. Can you park my car? I got held up and I am running late!" Phil was doing the varsity game and was definitely late. I said, "Sure, Phil" and he tossed me the keys and ran into the gym. Thirty minutes later, I secured my second spot of the day and parked Phil's car.

I caught the last few minutes of the first half of an exciting match-up. Then it was time for me to prepare for my game. The varsity guys game into the locker room, wished us luck, and off we went. Phil thanked me again, and we said goodbye.

Leadership Takeaway: You just never know. It could be the smallest thing, like someone asking you to park their car. I admired Phil, wanted to work the games like he did one day, and have that swagger like he did. Little did I know that after that quick interaction, Phil would take me under his wing. He guided me, became a mentor to me, assigned me games, and gave me some opportunities later down the road. What if I had hesitated, or said "No," or made up some lame excuse like, "I am not comfortable driving your car without the proper insurance"? Where would that relationship have gone?

Be authentic in your interactions with others. This was a right-time, right-place situation, and I responded with a simple, "Sure, Phil." Well, that was the start of a long mentorship—all with the flip of the keys. Phil was good to me all those years after that experience. I was grateful years later to be a mentor for Phil's son Phil, who became a successful Division I ref.

When the chance presents itself, help out your neighbor. Be ready.

96. The elbow.

November 11, 2010 University of Texas Longhorns vs. Louisiana Tech, Austin, Texas.

Early game in November. Texas was playing an underdog that they should have beaten easily. I had never been to Austin, Texas, before, and I was excited to be there. This was the year that the NCAA focused on the elbow hit to the head and the devastating play of an offensive player swinging his elbows with the chance of injuring a close defender. There was a heavy penalty of either a flagrant one technical foul or a flagrant two foul, which could eject the player from the game for hitting somebody with an elbow. Implementing this new safety rule was part of the NCAA planning meetings, it was part of the early-season training videos, and it was a point of emphasis for the upcoming season. It was heavily talked about within referee circles as well as the media.

The visiting team had come to play, and it was a competitive game throughout the first half. Late in the first half, an offensive player grabbed a rebound on the baseline and was trapped by two defenders. The player violently swung his elbow trying to clear space, striking the defender in the face. I was on the play. It happened right in front of me, and it was as if it were in slow motion. The defender fell backward, grabbing his face. It seemed like the world stopped watching, saying, "This is the elbow play they're talking about—the one we've been prepping for!"

I threw my fist in the air calling a foul enthusiastically, signaled the elbow play, and then pointed to the TV monitor that we were going to look at to review it.

I did call the play a flagrant one, and the player received a technical foul. The defensive man was awarded two free throws, *and* possession of the ball was awarded to the defensive team. It was a big moment for me and my crew, as it was one of the first plays to happen in a live NCAA Division I game that was nationally televised. I received many texts from fans, supervisors, and fellow officials who saw the play and congratulated me and the crew for "getting it right." It was a nice moment for me, and I enjoyed the fact that I did get the play right on the national stage.

Leadership Takeaway: You are prepared for the big moments that are coming. Regardless of your business or your work, there are new rules, new strategies, and new techniques that you prepare for. When they finally come your way and you can implement them as designed, it's a great feeling. Prepare yourself for these moments because you don't know when they will come. With proper preparation and a keen eye, you will see them, sense them, and get it right when it comes your way. I didn't know it at the time, but I had read the new rules so much that, when it happened, the whole situation slowed down right in front of my eyes. I was able to process it and then implement the rules as designed. It was quite a satisfying feeling. I wish you the best when that moment comes for you…and it will. #BeReady.

97. Mom's watching.

When my Dad passed away in 2008, I grew closer with my Mom. Mom has always been a big part of my life and always there for me, and this grew, even more, when Dad passed. She began to travel with me at least once a year to different cities and events: Duke, Williamsburg, D.C., Charleston, Syracuse, Boston, etc. I loved it all, and it was a fun time for both of us. She met the other officials, the supervisors, etc. She was so cute collecting the tickets from each game, finding her way to will-call, buying a koozie for me at each place, and certainly a nice meal after the game.

As Mom and I grew closer, she also became a bigger fan of the game. She just didn't casually watch anymore—she was watching what actually happened in the game: time, space, score, and type of play. She began to know and watch when I'd get a great play right or when I kicked one. It was kinda like she was reading my mind and hearing me talk to myself during the game.

Each year, I worked more and more games on TV. She'd text in the afternoon about where I was, and then get going on her routine: finding the channel, getting her dinner plans set. If she had gear from that school, she'd put it on; then she'd start calling her ever-growing circle of friends and families who also liked to watch my games. She knew she couldn't put anything in writing to anyone because of the confidentiality of the assignments, so she called each person, each night. It kept her in touch with her friends, and she enjoyed sharing the news of the games.

Leadership Takeaway: It was a nice feeling knowing that Mom was watching. I always wanted to do an outstanding job and get plays right, yet it was a little more special knowing that Mom and her circle of friends were watching. It was like she was there with me in a way. And not that I did anything different than I normally would, but it did add a little bit extra to my work. I wanted to make my Mom proud, so maybe, subconsciously, I wanted to be a little better on those nights.

Remember the bracelets, "WWJD"? What would Jesus do? People would wear them as a reminder to do good out in the world. When Mom was watching, I felt MWTGDG: "Mom's watching the game, do good!" How would you act if your Mom watched you at work? Studied your interactions with others and watched with a keen eye the decisions you made? I enjoyed the challenge and was glad Mom was watching. I was ready.

This continued with visits to my school in Port Jervis, New York, where I was Principal. She'd visit for a half a day, come to some classes, see the kids and staff, and again, watch me at work. I loved it and felt the proudest when people would tell her what a great job I was doing as Principal. Compliments are always nice, but when your Mom hears them about you, they're the best! Be ready to work like Mom is watching! Thanks, Mom, for being there on all those special trips! #She'sfromBoston.

---

98. Hot dog.

January 16, 2010 George Mason University (GMU) at James Madison University (JMU), Harrisonburg, Virginia.

A hot dog. Really? A hot dog on the court. I was always ready for anything, but I did not know what to do here. We were in the middle of a barn burner at JMU playing against in-state rival GMU. Place was packed and soooo loud. Intense environment for sure. JMU was making a comeback, and the crowd was crazed.

With the opportunity to cut the lead to three points, JMU went to the free-throw line. I was standing with my back to the crowd prepping for the free throw when I saw it. It was in slow motion, and (in my head) there was sound with it as it flew through the air. It was like a paper airplane in flight, slowly making its way to the runway, which was the court. Yes, the dog. The hot dog itself, with ketchup and mustard (one bite taken out of it) and the little paper tray it lay on.

The hot dog arrived, smashing onto the court right before the player from JMU shot the free throw. Pandemonium hit, and the place went wild. My team got together, talked it out, and, thankfully, my partner knew the rule. It was a challenge because at the moment on the court, you could *not* go review the rule book. You had to know it.

Leadership Takeaway: Be ready. When you have been doing something long enough, off-the-wall things will happen. This situation was certainly out of the ordinary, and I was not 100% sure of the rule at that moment.

This experience got my nose back into the rule book, not only to know the common rules inside and out, but to become more familiar with those less-common situations. It made me more aware of the "anything can happen" scenario and just more ready in general. It is funny how when you go through these types of experiences, you become better. I am grateful to my partner for knowing the rule in this situation.

Deeper reflection: I have thought about this play quite often, and it was talked about for a long time. Two things bothered me after I thought about it for a while:

1. How did we know it wasn't a visiting fan who put a home shirt on, walked down, and threw the hotdog, knowing it could hurt the home team? A little conspiracy-theory action, but it *could* happen, right? It was just a kid in a purple shirt, and it could have been anyone, yet the penalty went against JMU.

2. Something that happened from off the court affected something that happened on the court. The visiting team scored two points because of a fan. It just didn't sit right with me. At that moment, we had to follow the rules, but in a way, those players from JMU got robbed because of some knucklehead.

After this incident, I proposed some changes to the rules committee. I'm not sure if any action was ever taken on my suggestions, but at least I knew I'd be ready if something similar happened again. #Hotdog

Here is a *Washington Post* article on the game:

99. Act as if.

I had done a lot of scrimmage games, HS games, camp games, junior college games, Division III games, Division II games, and more before I reached the Division I level. Even at the Division I level, there is a big difference between some of the smaller venues/conferences and the five power conferences and the venues of these schools. I have written about this many times throughout this book and what it was like to be in those spaces: The Carrier Dome in Syracuse, Cameron Indoor Stadium at Duke, Madison Square Garden in New York City, etc. The bright lights and biggest stages. I'd always heard many of the older guys and supervisors ask, "But can he do it under the bright lights? On the big stage?" That is the question you have to answer for yourself.

Leadership Takeaway: None of it prepares you for those moments, and all of it does. Every little thing I did before I reached those venues helped get me ready, yet, when you first step into those spaces, it is all so new, so big, and so bright. Point: Work your tail off, and *act as if* you're under the bright lights. Create it in your head, mind, and heart that you are at the Garden tonight, and work *as if*. Do not confuse this with the concept of "Be where your feet are" or hoping you were somewhere else. *Acting as if* will help prepare you for when you do make it to the next level, to the bright lights.

The same is true with speaking gigs and keynoting: I have presented in many a classroom, auditorium, and cafeteria. But now I'm speaking in venues where I can't see the last person because they are so far away, and it is so big; I am ready. In all those prior presentations, I *acted as if* I were in those settings to prepare me to be under the bright lights. Every moment and none of the moments helped me when I landed in those spaces.

Take each opportunity as a learning experience to help prepare you for the #brightlights.

100. Big call, big stage, big confidence.

Written by Jose Anibal Carrion. Bilingual Teacher for 21 years, NCAA official for multiple DI conferences, FIBA, and Puerto Rican Pro league referee 20 + years. I am proud to say I worked my first DI game with Jose!

Sunday, August 15, 2004. Argentina vs. Serbia, Athens, Greece. The Olympics was the stage for the rematch between Argentina and Serbia (former Yugoslavia), who disrupted the Championship Game of the 2002 FIBA World Cup; Yugoslavia won that game, and it left a bad taste in the Argentinians' mouth. It was the second game of the day, the atmosphere was charged, and the game was intense, as expected. With 3.8 seconds left in the game and the game tied, Yugoslavia was fouled and given two free throws. The first throw was missed and the second made. Argentina inbounded the ball, and an alley-oop pass was thrown to Argentinian star Manu Ginobili, who was in the air. Manu barely grabbed the ball and threw it to the basket. The ball was in the air and the horn went off, the ball hit the glass and...went in! The trail official (the referee in the back of the play) was responsible to decide if the basket was good or not. This was me, and I scored it!! And chaos began!!!

Argentinians were running all over the court while Serbians were in disbelief. The angry Serbian coach was in front of me, yelling, "You can't score that—you must ask the Commissioner (person in charge of the Table Officials)!" Now, the Serbian coach was complaining at the Officials Table. Then, he went to my partner—who was the Crew Chief—and he came to me. "Are you sure?" he asked. I replied: "I am." He said, "Let's go to ask the Commissioner." I said, "Will do."

It has been 17 years since that monologue (I was the only one who talked), and the first time I will write or say what I said at that moment: "Sir, I am here because they want me to ask you. They can see me here, but I am *not* here to ask you. I am here to *tell* you that I am 100% sure that the basket is good and that the game is over."

I turned around. Looking at my partners, we left the scorer's table. In the meantime, the play was shown several times on the arena screen, and (Thank God) the video replay validated my judgment: the ball was away by inches of Ginobili's fingertips.

Leadership Takeaway: My first game could have been my last. A right decision followed by a strong leadership strategy to stay and believe in my decision moved me forward. I knew I had it right and was not going to allow someone else to seal my fate. I would live and die with the consequence of it all. This decision at that moment allowed me to have a successful rest of the Olympic tournament and future life as an International referee.

At the moment, I hustled down the court to get a great look, zeroed in my focus, slowed it down, and then emphatically scored the goal. I went with my gut, knew I was right, and told the Commissioner so. I am proud of my decision then and now. #Trustyourgut.

10
ABSORB THE CHAOS

Absorb chaos, create calm, and provide hope.
—J.D. Collins, NCAA National Coordinator

101. Absorbing chaos.

Written by J.D. Collins, National Coordinator of men's basketball officiating (2015). John is a tremendous leader, having officiated at the Division I level for eighteen years. He worked in the NCAA tournament for ten years, making the Final Four, Elite Eight, and multiple Sweet Sixteen appearances. He exudes calm under pressure, leadership, and confidence from his time on the court to now, in the *ultimate leadership position in NCAA officiating. A true leader, on and off the court.*

I was officiating the Big Ten men's basketball semi-final in March of 2004 between Michigan State and Wisconsin. It was an intense game, with plenty of drama. Late in the game, Coach Izzo disagreed vehemently with a call I had made. As my wife would later recount, Coach Izzo disagreed so much that he buried his head into my neck screaming at the top of his lungs. I adjudicated a bench decorum Class A technical foul on Coach Izzo for his actions. Michigan State lost by one to Wisconsin in that semi-final matchup.

Fast forward three and half weeks—I was fortunate to be selected as the alternate official for the Final Four in San Antonio. Duke, UConn, Georgia Tech, and Oklahoma State were playing in that Final Four. As the Alternate official, you are required to be onsite from Friday through Tuesday morning. On Sunday, the off day, my wife, Jennifer, and I went for a walk on the Riverwalk. First, the place was mobbed with people. Second, her walk turned into shopping. So, I ended up standing on one of the bridges that cross the Riverwalk, people watching. I had the opportunity to talk with many different people standing on that bridge. In addition, it was much less crowded on the bridges.

As I was people watching, I noticed Coach Izzo walking by with his wife. I scream at the top of my lungs, "Izzo, you suck! Izzo, you suck!" This got Coach Izzo's attention. He turned, saw me, and ran up to the top of the bridge to give me a congratulatory hug. He was truly proud of my advancement. As we were embracing, my wife was walking up the bridge behind me. She saw Coach Izzo hugging me and said, "I don't understand—this is the guy that was

Absorb the Chaos

'buried in you' three weeks ago. I introduced my wife to Coach Izzo, and he shared how excited he was for my success.

In officiating, there is a huge difference between people "liking you" and people "respecting you." Earning respect comes over the long haul. We, as officials, don't really care if people like us—we just want them to respect the job we do. Our job as officials and in life is to absorb chaos, create calm, and provide hope. If you could see a picture of that moment between coach Izzo and me, you would see him out of control and me with a poised and in-control look on my face.

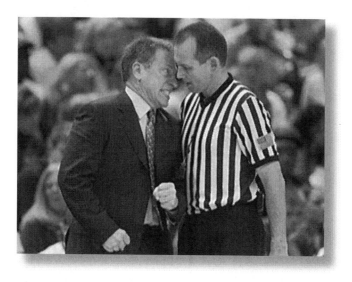

Leadership Takeaways:

1. *Work hard* at having people respect you, and pay less attention to whether they like you or not. This perspective is more sustainable in leadership.

2. *Absorb chaos*—In today's society, there are too many divisions—racial, medical, pandemic, and political to name a few. Our job in life is to absorb chaos for those with whom we interact. We shouldn't make assumptions on what is going on with them. The reality is that we all have something big going on! Our leadership role is to absorb part of their chaos and be good listeners. This may give us the opportunity to speak into their lives—and make a difference.

3. *Create calm*—have you ever tried to talk rationally with someone who is not calm? So many people are in the middle of chaos, and they just need someone to model for them how to approach the problem in a calm manner. Secondarily, when we provide calm for someone, they are more likely to listen to us because calm is what they desire.

4. *Provide hope*—without hope, you have nothing. For a basketball coach, the hope is that during the last two minutes of the game, they are going to get a fair shake (not get screwed) by the officials. In life, people just want to know that there is still hope. That is one of the biggest threats to our society—people are losing hope. As leaders, we have the opportunity to share hope with our constituents. Don't undervalue the opportunity you have to share hope with each person you interact with today!

Absorb chaos, create calm, and provide hope!
—J.D. Collins

Conclusion
THE LAST WHISTLE

The last whistle.

Many times when I completed my job as a ref, people were unhappy in some way. It was just part of the game. I hope that is not the case here and that you enjoyed this journey with me. Through all the ups and downs, I did enjoy it. Looking back at so many of the experiences written here, there were an abundance of amazing people who touched my heart and mind along the way. The power of a single interaction can leave such a lasting impact on others. Think about that as you grow along your own journey. I tried to highlight this point throughout the book.

Mistakes, failures, and the grind of so many games are part of the journey, but those are not what stick with me. It is the relationships and tremendous experiences that I had that stick. Those are the important things that stay with me all these years later.

As I make the last call on *Tales from the Hardwood*, it is my true goal that these stories had a positive impact on your life and that you will grow from them. Become a better spouse, parent, leader, educator, coach, and official. This book isn't just for officials, but for anyone looking to grow in their leadership journey. I wish you the best in your journey. #survivethrive #keeprolling

About the Author
ANDREW MAROTTA

Andrew Marotta is the enthused and energetic Principal at Port Jervis Middle School, located in beautiful Port Jervis, New York. He served sixteen years as HS Principal and Assistant Principal. Under his collaborative leadership, Port Jervis HS grew in many areas, including academic achievement, student success, and most importantly, a culture of #PortPride. He loves his school community and continues to #survivethrive in his efforts to continue to move things forward.

Andrew is supported by his loving family, his wife Jennifer, and his children, Claire, Matthew, and Tessa. So many experiences in this book are from Andrew's role as a Principal, a son, and his favorite role, being a dad to his wonderful children. He is so grateful for his family and loves them unconditionally.

In addition to *Tales from the Hardwood*, Andrew has authored his first book, *The Principal: Surviving and Thriving* in 2017, 2nd edition, *The School Leader*, in 2020. He released a guide for success for parents and educators entitled *The Partnership* in 2020. These books have propelled Andrew to become a national speaker and presenter on leadership, relationship building, and the points of his logo: energy, enthusiasm, effort, extra—all leading to excellence. He is a master storyteller who brings his audiences to laugh, cry, think, reflect and more. He is truly proud to share his experiences from his time on the court as a leader and Division I men's basketball official in *Tales from the Hardwood, Surviving and Thriving*.

Learn more about Andrew at https://andrewmarotta.com/ Sign up for his weekly leadership blog #ELBlog on his website, and watch his podcast on social media #ELB Education Leadership and Beyond. He truly is AlottaMarotta! Reach out to him on twitter @andrewmarotta21.

#SurviveThrive

Made in the USA
Middletown, DE
05 May 2025

75073626R00125